Humanism of the Other

Humanism
of the Other

EMMANUEL LÉVINAS

Translated from the French
by Nidra Poller

Introduction
by Richard A. Cohen

University of Illinois Press
Urbana and Chicago

First paperback edition, 2006
Humanisme de l'autre homme © 1972 by Éditions Fata Morgana
English translation and introduction © 2003 by the Board of Trustees
of the University of Illinois
All rights reserved
Manufactured in the United States of America
1 2 3 4 5 C P 6 5 4 3

∞ This book is printed on acid-free paper.

The essays in *Humanisme de l'autre homme* first appeared in
the following publications: "La Signification et le Sens," *Revue
de métaphysique et de morale,* 1964; "Humanisme et an-archie,"
Revue internationale de philosophie, 1968; "Sans identité,"
L'Éphémère, 1970.

The Library of Congress cataloged the cloth edition as follows:
Lévinas, Emmanuel.
[Humanisme de l'autre homme. English.]
Humanism of the other / Emmanuel Levinas ; translated from
the French by Nidra Poller ; introduction by Richard A. Cohen.
p. cm.
Includes bibliographical references and index.
ISBN 0-252-02840-6 (alk. paper)
1. Humanism. 2. Intersubjectivity. 3. Meaning (Philosophy)
4. Culture—Philosophy. I. Poller, Nidra. II. Title.
B2430.L48H8413   2003
133—dc21   2002151569

PAPERBACK ISBN 978-0-252-07326-7

Contents

Introduction:
Humanism and Anti-humanism—
Levinas, Cassirer, and Heidegger

Richard A. Cohen

The resurrection is not the rise of the dead from their tombs but
the passage from the death of self-absorption to the life of unselfish
love, the transition from the darkness of selfish individualism to
the light of universal spirit, from falsehood to truth, from the
slavery of the world to the liberty of the eternal.

—Savepalli Radhakrishnan (1936)

We know that as a graduate student Emmanuel Levinas attended the
now famous 1929 Davos debate between Ernst Cassirer and Martin Heidegger. We have not sufficiently appreciated the importance of this debate for Levinas's thought.

The debate between Cassirer and Heidegger, more often implicit
than explicit, extended far beyond their personal encounter at Davos,
Switzerland, in the spring of 1929. So, too, it signified far more than a
debate about Kant or the academic discipline of philosophy. Indeed,
the importance of the longer Cassirer-Heidegger debate, extending
from the 1920s to the 1940s—from Cassirer's three-volume *Philosophy of Symbolic Forms* (1923, 1925, 1929)[1] to his last completed book, *An
Essay on Man* (1944),[2] and from Heidegger's monumental *Being and
Time* (1927)[3] to his "Letter on Humanism" (1946/47)[4]—concerns more
than just the confrontation between two versions of Kant and philosophy, a cosmopolitan "philosophy of culture" on the one side and the
Seinsfrage ("question of being"), the critique of "the metaphysics of
presence," on the other. It also represents a clash between humanism
and anti-humanism and a debate over the meaning of the West.

Levinas's own brand of humanism appears throughout his writings but especially in the three chapters—"Signification and Sense" (1964),[5] "Humanism and An-archy" (1968),[6] and "Without Identity" (1970)[7]— collected in 1972 in the present volume, which Levinas entitled *Humanism of the Other* (*Humanisme de l'autre homme*).[8] This humanism must be understood within the intellectual and spiritual context and parameters established by the twentieth century's profound and far-reaching debate over the nature of philosophy and the worth of humanism. It is a debate of many acts, with many contributors and interlocutors, but its true depths are plumbed in the philosophical and personal confrontation between Cassirer and Heidegger.

Note that these chapters were written and published as separate articles before, during, and after the turbulent student protests in Paris known as "May 1968." Note, too, and even more powerfully, the larger historical backdrop of Soviet and Maoist totalitarianism, the mass slaughter of World Wars I and II, the twelve-year reign of Nazi terror, the million Jewish children and 5 million Jewish adults murdered in the Holocaust, and the atomic bombings of Hiroshima and Nagasaki. The twentieth century, for all its scientific and technical advances, was perhaps the bloodiest in human history. Levinas responds not only to the long philosophical tradition and its most contemporary philosophical developments but also and poignantly to the political situation of twentieth-century France, Europe, and the world.

Are we to forget that Levinas spent the war years in a prisoner-of-war work camp for Jewish French soldiers or that his parents, siblings, and millions of his coreligionists were murdered by the Nazis? Surely Levinas did not. His second major work, *Otherwise than Being or Beyond Essence* (1974),[9] bears the following dedication: "To the closest among the six million murdered by the National Socialists, side by side with the millions and millions of all confessions and all nations who were victims of the same hatred of the other, the same anti-Semitism." But Levinas returns love for hate, the "wisdom of love," the "humanism of the other," against the "hatred of the other"—a hard love, yes, a "difficult freedom," no doubt, but the subtleties no less than the brutalities of contemporary anti-humanism have never been more sophisticated.

The three chapters of *Humanism of the Other* each defend human-ism—the worldview founded on the belief in the irreducible dignity of humans, a belief in the efficacy and worth of human freedom and hence also of human responsibility—from different angles. Each argues against different philosophical positions, all of which would reduce the human to the inhuman.

In "Signification and Sense," published a few years after his first masterwork, *Totality and Infinity* (1961),[10] but already anticipating the close analyses of *Otherwise than Being*, Levinas subtly discusses the origin of meaning and its relation to cultural symbols. Here the opponent is the philosophy of culture articulated by Cassirer, although Levinas never mentions him by name. I will return to this chapter later.

"Humanism and An-archy," while clearly having the events of May 1968 in view, targets the structuralism of Claude Lévi-Strauss and Michel Foucault. Taking the term *anarchy* in its etymological sense of "no principle (*anarchē*)," no Archimedean point, Levinas reveals and challenges the dehumanization perpetrated by all the "social sciences" that seek to explain away human subjectivity in the name of abstract *principles*, the "intelligible structures" wherein subjectivity "would have no internal finality."[11]

Framed by the same intellectual backdrop, "Without Identity" continues to oppose structuralism, with its then intellectually fashionable slogan of the "death of the subject," in the name of the irrepressible "youth" of ethical responsibility, the "sincerity," "frankness," and "authenticity" of genuine concern for the other. In the street protests and alleged anarchy of the student revolt, Levinas sees the uncorrupted moral and political idealism of youth. In this chapter, however, the philosophical opponent is not simply French structuralism or an effort to discover a core of idealism within ideology but also Heidegger, whose "fundamental ontology" submerges human subjectivity in the impersonal historical "truth of being." Throughout his entire intellectual career, Levinas—and Cassirer as well—is stimulated and provoked by Heidegger's ontological reduction of the human, his philosophical adulation of being, to the articulation and defense of the irreducible human dimension of signification.

Davos, 1929: Culture versus Being

By 1929, in addition to being recognized as original and distinguished philosophers, both Cassirer and Heidegger were also recognized as Kant scholars. Cassirer's credentials were impeccable. While still at university he studied under the great neo-Kantian Hermann Cohen. From 1912 to 1918 he had served as the general editor of a definitive eleven-volume edition of the complete works of Kant; he was also the individual editor or coeditor of four of the eleven volumes in this edition.[12] In 1918, at the end of this enormous scholarly labor and more than a decade before Davos, he published his own magisterial intellectual biography of Kant, entitled *Kants Leben und Lehre (Kant's Life and Thought)*.[13] As for Heidegger, in 1929, shortly before the Davos debate, he published his own original Kant book, *Kant und das Problem der Metaphysik (Kant and the Problem of Metaphysics)*,[14] which knit Kant's critique of reason into his own existential and ontological project articulated several years earlier in *Being and Time*. After their debate, in 1931, Cassirer published a highly critical review of Heidegger's Kant book.[15]

On one level the 1929 Davos encounter was a scholarly debate, pitting two incompatible interpretations of Kant against each other.[16] More specifically, the debate opposed two comprehensive and incompatible interpretations of the role of *imagination* and *reason* within the overall architecture of Kant's *Critique of Pure Reason*. On another level, however, it was a philosophical debate between Heidegger and Cassirer. On the one side, *Kant and the Problem of Metaphysics* was in truth an original and idiosyncratic continuation or application of the "*Dasein* analysis"[17] that Heidegger had earlier articulated in *Being and Time;* on the other, Cassirer, too, had already articulated his own way of understanding Kant in the three volumes of his *Philosophy of Symbolic Forms*. Thus the Davos encounter, beyond being simply a matter of Kant scholarship, an "*explication de texte,*" was also a collision between the whole of Heidegger's philosophy of being and the whole of Cassirer's philosophy of culture. That is how both Heidegger and Cassirer understood their debate, and, to speak more objectively, it is how the debate was understood by those who attended.

This debate clearly shows that Cassirer, independent of his own particular philosophical point of view, was greatly concerned to get Kant right—that is, to be a conscientious and faithful Kant scholar. There can be little doubt that Cassirer's Kant, unlike Heidegger's Kant, is faithful to the text of Kant himself. As I will show, however, this very difference reflects an essential dimension of the confrontation between Cassirer and Heidegger. It raises the question of *truth* and *method:* How should one read or appropriate the works of other philosophers or cultural artifacts more generally, up to and including the entire spiritual heritage of the West (and now, one might add, of the world at large)? How does one encounter the other? How does one preserve ineradicable differences while at the same time make genuine contact? It is a question as old as philosophy, a mystery as ancient as religion: the problem of identity and difference, the one and the many. Putting the issue of their different philosophical approaches in a preliminary way, Cassirer defended the possibility, across discourse, of discovering the "infinity," "ideality," or "objectivity" of cultural formations. Heidegger, in contrast, defended the necessity of a steadfast return to the "finitude," or historical situation, of all that is meaningful.

It is of more than casual interest that both thinkers understood Heidegger's approach as a violation of the text or at least of its relation to the author's intention. For Heidegger, however, this violence was both necessary and productive, an indication of the intellectual effort required to return a text from a merely subjective context—including the entire realm of theoretical objectivity—to its "essential" relation to its ground in being. For Cassirer, this same violence represented Heideggerian ontology's colossal failure to provide any objective standards for life and thought. In his private notes jotted down during the Davos debate, Cassirer tellingly wrote: "Heidegger speaks here not as a commentator but as a usurper."[18] Already, then, the weight of the entire debate between Cassirer and Heidegger, a debate between the conflicting perspectives of humanism and anti-humanism, is contained and revealed in these two different ways of reading, these two ways of understanding the other.

The intricacies of Kant interpretation are not my primary concern. In each instance, however, it is clear that the disagreements regarding fine points of Kant interpretation reveal more profoundly the irreconcilable opposition between the larger worldviews of Cassirer and Heidegger.

Heidegger's reading of Kant focuses primarily on the imagination. He proposes that the heart of Kant's *Critique of Pure Reason* lies in the central role of the imagination as the link between sensible existence, on the one side, and the syntheses of understanding and the unifying idealism of reason, on the other. What is more profoundly at stake is a defense of the finitude of *Dasein* as propounded in *Being and Time.* By linking reason and understanding to sensible existence via an existential interpretation of the imagination, one that characterizes it in terms of the mood (*Stimmung*) and ecstatic temporality of *Dasein,* and then understanding moodful and temporal *Dasein*'s "fate" (*Schicksal*) as "thrown" (*geworfen*) into the "destiny" (*Geschick*) of the history of being, Heidegger challenges what for Cassirer, along with most Kant interpreters, is Kant's altogether different commitment to the Enlightenment ideal of the infinity of reason as a guide regulating the understanding, even if the understanding is indeed bound to sensibility via the imagination. By reading Kant's work from the bottom up, understanding finite sensibility as its terminus a quo and terminus ad quem, Heidegger is arguing that Kant's *Critique* is an ontology, indeed, an ontology rooted in the finitude of *Dasein* and historical being. Cassirer, however, reads the *Critique* from the top down, from its *terminus ad quem* in reason's ideal of unity and, beyond that, from the viewpoint of the ethical and aesthetic ideals opened up by the dialectical distinction between appearances and the "thing-in-itself"—that is, he reads it as it is usually read and as Kant himself interpreted it in his *Prologomena to Any Future Metaphysics.* According to this reading, what defines Kant's project in the first critique is not ontology but epistemology, the "theory of knowledge."[19] The Davos dispute over the nature and status of imagination in Kant's *Critique of Pure Reason* was in truth a radical confrontation over the nature and role of *reason* in relation to finite humanity. Is reason the highest unifying guide or the thinnest abstract derivative of human existence? For Heidegger, reason is a derivative construct whose original sense must be discovered in the existential structures of *Dasein* and hence in *Dasein*'s ground within historical being. For Cassirer, to the contrary, reason is the *raison d'être* of humanity as a rational animal, the guiding and unifying consciousness presiding over all meaning formations. The differences between these two readings of Kant bear enormous consequences for a conception of freedom and hence for an understanding of humanism.

Freedom for Heidegger is, first, *Dasein*'s freedom to appropriate the finitude of its fate and its place within its historical destiny. Freedom is thus a combination of "resoluteness" and "enrootedness"—resolute enrootedness in finitude. Second, and more profoundly, it is *being's* freedom to reveal (as well as simultaneously to conceal) its epochal donation of meaning, a generosity to which the thinker, that is, Heidegger, must receptively attend in a thankful listening rather than in the usual willful interference. By means of this interpretation of finite freedom, Heidegger devotes his entire philosophical effort to reversing the famous "Copernican revolution" of Kant's thought. Deeper than all the relative ends constructed by consciousness, whether practical or theoretical, is the bestowal of meaning that comes not from humans but from being. Human rules are ruled by being.

For Cassirer, freedom remains very much within the orbit of Kant's Copernican revolution. Freedom is, first, humanity's capacity to objectify meanings through the symbol-forming character of consciousness, that is, through the production of the cultural environment that is the uniquely human realm. Humanity freely produces meaning not merely through the cognition of scientific objects or through a rational ethics or aesthetics but also—and here Cassirer creatively broadens Kant's more abstract notion of rationality by integrating the contributions of language and culture—through the symbol formations of myth, art, language, and religion as well as science. In contrast to Heidegger, who characterizes the human as inextricably mortal or finite, Cassirer sees the human as uniquely the *animal symbolicum*—the symbol-forming animal. Second, as the task of philosophy, freedom is humanity's ability and responsibility to become increasingly self-conscious and hence increasingly enlightened regarding the universality of its powers and products of symbolic construction. Freedom is guided by the ideal of self-consciousness, self-knowledge, humanity made aware of its own meaning production. In the opening sentence of *An Essay on Man*, a work that in many way summarizes and concludes *The Philosophy of Symbolic*

Forms, Cassirer declares unequivocally that "self-knowledge is the highest aim of philosophical inquiry."[20] "We must try to break the chain connecting us with the outer world," he continues, "in order to enjoy our true freedom."[21] The rules of humanity rule an unruly nature.

Thus their discussion of Kant already shows the grounds for the radical disagreement between Cassirer and Heidegger regarding humanism. For the one, human freedom is self-consciousness, self-knowledge, the recognition, in close examination of cultural products, of consciousness as the transcendental source of meaning. For the other, freedom is not even human but requires of the human a resolute but humble receptivity, a careful disengagement from human willfulness for the sake of a correct placement within what is the freedom of being's generosity as the source of meaning.

Cassirer, Heidegger, and the Third Reich

Perhaps life can be separated from philosophy, but a philosopher cannot be separated from his or her life. Neither Cassirer, in the name of culture, nor Heidegger, in the name of being, nor Levinas, in the name of moral judgment, would permit any such personal evasion.

It cannot in good conscience remain unsaid that in May 1933, just four years after their Davos encounter, Cassirer, who had been appointed the first Jewish rector of the University of Marburg, had to flee with his wife and child from Germany under pressure of Nazi persecution. Heidegger, by then a member of the Nazi Party, accepted the rectorship of the University of Freiburg, delivering his infamous inaugural address endorsing the Nazi program. Cassirer's tribulations and forced peregrinations to England, Sweden, and finally the United States and his uninterrupted and noble manifestation of the highest human values in his own person and work are by now well known, if perhaps insufficiently appreciated, as are Heidegger's Nazi affiliation—from 1933 to 1945—and his unapologetic silence thereafter regarding his own role in and the significance (let alone the existence) of the Third Reich and the Holocaust.

Levinas attended the Davos debate in 1929 as a young graduate assistant, doing so at the invitation of Heidegger. Levinas also participated in a short student play mocking the debate, a farce attended by all the participants, including Heidegger, Cassirer, and Cassirer's wife. Powdering his hair white, Levinas played Cassirer. In a short interview with Roger-Pol Droit, published in *Le Monde* on 2 June 1992, more than sixty years later,[22] Levinas concludes with a "brief recollection" of Davos. I cite it in full.

> During the summer [actually spring] of 1929 I attended the celebrated Davos meeting, which was marked by the philosophical opposition between Ernst Cassirer and Martin Heidegger. As you know, it was following this historic confrontation that the thoughts inspired by Kant and the heritage of the Enlightenment, primarily represented by Cassirer, disappeared from Germany. Now, one evening, during this gathering, we put on a revue, a small play, which Cassirer and Heidegger attended, where we mimicked their controversy. For my part, I played (*j'incarnais*) Cassirer, whose positions Heidegger constantly attacked. And to convey Cassirer's noncombative and somewhat woebegone attitude, I continually repeated: "I am a pacifist."[23]

Three comments. First, to my knowledge it is only in this late interview and in one other interview (conducted by François Poirié a few years earlier, in 1986)[24] that Levinas mentions Cassirer by name. Cassirer's name never appears in any of Levinas's many published writings, even in *Humanism of the Other;* where Cassirer's philosophy of culture is implicitly discussed and criticized. Perhaps Levinas wanted to distance himself from the neo-Kantianism of Hermann Cohen (who is also rarely mentioned in Levinas's writings) and Cassirer precisely because of his closeness to it, although this is mere speculation. Second, despite this formal absence, Cassirer is nevertheless very present in Levinas's thinking, as is clearly the case in "Signification and Sense." Third, and here again I am speculating, I believe that Levinas quickly came to regret his part in the student revue and that his regret stayed with him for a lifetime. According to the personal testimony of Professor Richard Sugarman, when Levinas came to the United States in 1973 as a visiting professor, he inquired of the whereabouts of Mrs. Cassirer, so that he might be able, in his own words, "to ask pardon of her"—forty years afterward. In his interview with Poirié, Levinas concludes his recollection of Davos as follows: "And then when Hitler came to power I

couldn't forgive myself [*je m'en suis beaucoup voulu*] for favoring Heidegger at Davos."[25]

Humanism and Anti-humanism:
Sartre, Heidegger, and Cassirer

Questions regarding the meaning and status of humanism have been
addressed from ancient Athens and Jerusalem, to the Christian Renaissance in Italy, and to the twentieth and twenty-first centuries. In
1945 and 1946 three figures and three texts stand out in the debate over
humanism. Because of the scale of its inhumanity, the twentieth century, perhaps more than any other, provoked a particularly thorough
and painstaking reexamination of the nature and worth of the human.

On the side of humanism, there is Cassirer's entire oeuvre, especially
his final works of the 1940s: *The Logic of the Humanities* (1942);[26] *An
Essay on Man,* written and published in English in 1945; and his posthu-
mously published book *The Myth of the State* (1945),[27] which addresses
fascist ideology. On this side, too, stands Jean-Paul Sartre's celebrated
essay "Existentialism Is a Humanism," written and published in French
in 1946. On the side of what Levinas calls "anti-humanism," there is
Heidegger's "Über den Humanismus" ("Letter on Humanism"), addressed to Jean Beaufret in Paris in 1946 and published in French (as
"Lettre sur l'humanisme") in an expanded version in 1947. Again on the
side of humanism are all of Levinas's works, but especially the present
volume, *Humanism of the Other,* published more than twenty-five years
after Sartre's essay and Heidegger's letter and offering an even more radical defense of humanism.

Sartre must be included in the debate over humanism not only because of his explicit and much-discussed defense of humanism in "Existentialism Is a Humanism" but also because, as do Heidegger and
Levinas, he begins with the phenomenological philosophy of Edmund
Husserl. His early philosophical work *The Transcendence of the Ego*
(1937), originally subtitled *A Sketch of a Descriptive Phenomenology*
(and finally subtitled *An Existentialist Theory of Consciousness*),[28] proposed an original interpretation of Husserl's transcendental ego. This
theory of self subsequently determined what became the bible of ex-

istentialism, Sartre's *Being and Nothingness,* published in 1943 during France's Nazi collaboration.[29]

Despite the common perception that Sartre is rooted in the concrete, especially as a self-proclaimed existentialist, one quickly discovers to the contrary that his philosophy is a highly abstract and severely rationalist "consciousness philosophy." The basis of all Sartre's thought depends on a clever but simplistic interpretation of the Husserlian transcendental ego that strips it of all content, leaving a pure self-reflective consciousness in its stead. It is this pure self-reflective consciousness, this fission of a self that is separated from itself by nothing but consciousness, by the very nothingness of a fully transparent self-consciousness, that Sartre takes to be the very definition of the human. When Sartre famously declares that "existence precedes essence," he does not mean by *existence* the variegated worldly being within which subjectivity is implicated and to which Heidegger, Cassirer, and Levinas devote lengthy descriptions. Rather, he means the pure freedom of self-reflective consciousness. Existence precedes essence because the nothingness or "freedom" of consciousness precedes the meanings—or essences—produced by that consciousness. Existence for Sartre is no more than the ecstatic but empty separation of consciousness from itself.

The Sartrean self is not a concrete self-in-the-world but rather the reflective consciousness of that self-in-the-world as a meaning projected by its own reflective consciousness. It is located in a pure distance from the world, a pure freedom of meaning projection, the nothingness rather than the being of *Being and Nothingness.* Sartre's philosophical universe is a sharply bifurcated intellectual abstraction: on the one side, the "for-itself," the pure activity of meaning projection, a nothingness or "freedom," and on the other, the "in-itself," the opaque being on which constituted meanings, "essences," are projected. When Sartre writes that subjectivity is "condemned to freedom," it means nothing more than that the subject, condemned forever to be for-itself, is the source of all meanings.

This bifurcated and abstract universe of the for-itself opposed to the in-itself, of pure freedom opposed to pure being, explains why the question of humanism is pressing for Sartre: how can the self as a for-itself, the source of all meaning, be said to be in communion with others, with humanity at large? Is not the self as a for-itself, source of all meaning, as much condemned to being alone as it is condemned to freedom? Is not the for-itself an absolute egology with no exit? Sartre writes "Existentialism Is a Humanism" precisely to address and solve this problem. At first sight, it seems that the humanism of Sartre's existentialism is obvious and unquestionable for, as he says in this essay: "Man is nothing else but that which he makes of himself" and therefore "man is responsible for what he is."[30] With regard to the individual human's serving as the source of meaning, contrary to Heidegger's claim that being is the source of meaning, or the structuralist claim that meaning derives from a network of signifiers constituted by the internal logic of language and culture, Sartre's proposal certainly stands on the side of humanism. And there is little doubt that Sartre the man, the "engaged" philosopher, was on the side of humanism. The problem, however, concerns human solidarity. Humanism, after all, is not merely the affirmation of the dignity of one person, of each individual alone; it is also an affirmation of the dignity of all humanity, the affirmation of an interhuman morality, community, and social justice. If the for-itself is the source of *all* meaning, then what possible significance can another human being have except either as an internal meaning projected by the for-itself, hence no longer as *another* person, or as a completely heteronomous and hence absolutely exterior opponent?

In "Existentialism Is a Humanism" Sartre attempts to overcome this dilemma by claiming to mean not "that he [the for-itself] is responsible only for his own individuality, but that he is responsible for all men." This constitutes Sartre's best *philosophical* attempt to defend an existential humanism. But according to Sartre's own dualistic philosophy, the expression "all men" can be only a meaning produced by and remaining within the freedom of a solitary for-itself. Given the absolute freedom Sartre accords to the for-itself, his further claim that "in choosing for himself he chooses for all men" cannot be distinguished from the absolute monarchical and totalitarian claim that one person chooses for all.[31] In the bright light of his own philosophy, the "other" for Sartre can be only a meaning projected by the self. To the for-itself, which is forever only for-itself, the "otherness" of the other person necessarily remains immanent, with the other never attaining the status of transcendent interlocutor. The self is free, to be sure, and the source of meaning, but at the price of being alone. If each person produces and is responsible for all meaning—is "condemned to be free,"[32] to use Sartre's expression—each person is at the same time no less condemned to his or her own world of meaning, his or her own solipsism. Sartre's existentialism is not and cannot be a humanism insofar as human community and social justice are necessary components of a genuine humanism. Despite his good intentions, Sartre, without the possibility of a theory of social interaction other than the war of each against all, is forced to admit of social life nothing more exalted than "Hell is other people."

Heidegger: A Letter from Being

In his "Letter on Humanism" Heidegger mentions and swiftly dismisses Sartre's reflections on existentialism and humanism. He does not precisely raise the criticism that I have raised—namely, the charge of solipsism. Rather, Heidegger criticizes Sartre's existentialism and alleged humanism because they have "not the least thing in common"[33] with the ontological notion of existence that guides Heidegger's reflections in *Being and Time* and elsewhere. Existence for Heidegger means ecstatic involvement in the world, not simply self-consciousness raised to its limit. Sartre's existentialism is for Heidegger but another example of the millennial tradition of Western "metaphysics in the oblivion of the truth of Being."[34] Several allusions in Heidegger's letter make it clear, too, that Cassirer's philosophy of culture would be yet another example of this oblivion. What, then, is the "truth of Being," and how does it guide Heidegger's thinking vis-à-vis humanism?

As I have already shown regarding his Kant interpretation, Heidegger saw the existence of *Dasein* as essentially "thrown" (*geworfen*) in the world: from the bottom, via the mood and temporality of *Dasein*'s mortal embodiment; from the middle, in its instrumental world of praxis; and from the top, in the derivative character of the intellectual constructions of theorizing consciousness. To say that *Dasein* is thrown in the world, however, has a very special significance for Heidegger. It means that temporal *Dasein* is thrown as a fate into the destiny or "historicity" (*Geschichtlichkeit*) of being—and *there* finds or is assigned its meaning. The key to Heidegger's thought, its distinctiveness, lies in its effort to reverse Kant's "Copernican revolution." Initiative regarding the emergence of meaning lies not with the human—whether as Sartre's monadic for-itself or across the vast cultural productions of Cassirer's *animal symbolicum*—but with being. Meaning is "being's move" (*le geste d'être*), to use Levinas's reformulation of Heidegger's basic thought, not humanity's. As Heidegger says: "Insofar as he ex-sists, man endures the 'being-there' by taking the There as the clearing of Being within his 'care.' The *Dasein* itself, however, is essentially the 'thrown.' It is essentially in the cast of Being, a destiny that destines, projects a destiny."[35] Meaning, or the "truth of Being," is not therefore a production of humanity; rather, humanity as mortal existence participates in—is thrown into—the "destiny" that is given by historical being.

The task of the philosopher, the authentic human being, is neither to project meaning existentially nor to re-present meaning intellectually, which tasks are "mere willing," "domination," and "decadence,"[36] but rather to hearken attentively to the meaning that is given by being. To give the human priority over being is but to darken and occlude being—to produce mere metaphysics, the subjective exaltation of this or that being (idea, form, substance, ego, etc.) over being. Heidegger announces the "end of metaphysics": being, not humanity, gives meaning. Humans, and foremost the thinker, must henceforth enter into the true calling of thought: listening to being. "The *it gives* rules as the destiny of Being." Heidegger declares, "Its history finds expression in the words of the essential thinkers. So the thought that thinks of the truth of Being thinks historically."[37] "Man is the guardian of Being,"[38] but only insofar as he is the mouthpiece of being. "Thus, what matters in the determination of the humanity of man as ex-sistence is not that man is the essential, but that Being is the essential."[39]

Heidegger rejects the traditional vision of humanism for which the human is central. It seems like little more than a play on words when, after having criticized all known versions of humanism as merely metaphysical, that is, instances of humanity's arrogantly displacing the "truth of Being," he nevertheless appropriates the term *humanism* to characterize his own ontology. (The context of this letter is the French discus-

sion of humanism, more specifically, Jean Beaufret's request that Heidegger clarify his own position vis-à-vis the meaning and value of humanism.) Heidegger writes—without much conviction, one senses—of
the humanism of his own thinking, or rather, of the humanism of the
thinking of the truth of being:

> Does it not think of this *humanitas* in such a decisive meaning as no meta-
> physics has thought or even can think of it? Is not this "humanism" in
> an extreme sense? Certainly. It is the humanism that thinks of the hu-
> manity of man from the nearness to Being.[40]

> "Humanism" means now, *should we decide to retain the word:* the essence
> of man is essential for the truth of Being, and *apart from this truth of Being
> man himself does not matter.*[41]

Such, then, is the humanism—or rather, the anti-humanism—of Heidegger's ontological redeployment of humanity in relation to being,
reversing Kant's Copernican revolution. There is no thesis about which
Heidegger is more insistent. The "greatest danger" facing humanity is
the failure to achieve this reversal. Nothing—not World War II, not the
Nazis, not the Holocaust—is more important than turning from
human self-centeredness, of which humanism is but an instance, to the
transcendence of being in its historical revelations, humbly and grate-
fully attending to *its* "giving" of meaning.

Cassirer Criticizes Heidegger

From their very first encounter at Davos, Cassirer contested Heidegger's
vision of man as thrown and, as such, delivered to the destiny of the truth
of being. Indeed, criticism of Heidegger's interpretation of the human
as *geworfen* is a constant throughout Cassirer's writings. Undoubtedly,
Cassirer acknowledged the phenomenological validity of certain of Heidegger's analyses regarding the existential character of human being.
After all, like Heidegger and Levinas, Cassirer is a "contemporary" philosopher, and the recognition of the inescapable and positive role of time,
language, and worldly being are part and parcel of contemporary philosophy. The third volume of *The Philosophy of Symbolic Forms,* for instance, is explicitly named *The Phenomenology of Knowledge.* Cassirer

fully recognizes the temporal, embodied, and worldly character of human being. Nevertheless, he views humanity's existential situation as a *terminus a quo* and not determinative of its *terminus ad quem*. What troubles Cassirer in Heidegger's interpretation of thrownness as the unsurpassable fate of all of *Dasein*'s endeavors insofar as they are beholden to the truth or destiny of historical being is this notion's negative consequences for any theory of epistemological validity and for any moral or "idealistic" outlook for politics. If humanity is trapped in the history of being, then history, not universal standards of truth or morality, rules human destiny. Does not Heidegger's ontology reduce to yet another pompous philosophy—like Hegel's, Marx's, or Spencer's—groveling at the feet of success, beholden to history's victors at the expense of the vanquished, now couched in the mysterious name of the "truth of being"? Cassirer says it does.

Indeed, in *The Myth of the State*, which is devoted to unmasking the mythological dimensions of twentieth-century fascism, Cassirer writes: "A theory that sees in the *Geworfenheit* of man one of his principal characters [has] given up all hope of an active share in the construction and reconstruction of man's cultural life. Such a philosophy renounces its own fundamental theoretical and ethical ideals. It can be used, then, as a pliable instrument in the hands of political leaders."[42] Having understood the human as thrown into and beholden to the truth of being, Heidegger has given up the essential dignity—the essential freedom—of the human that is the hallmark of all humanism. The first chapter of Cassirer's *Essay on Man* is entitled "The Crisis in Man's Knowledge of Himself." Whereas Heidegger claims the greatest danger of our time to lie in our usurpation of being's initiative, Cassirer sees the crisis of our time as precisely the reverse, namely, the view that our "claim to being the center of the universe has lost its foundation."[43] Cassirer calls for not less responsibility for truth, morality, and justice but more—humanity taking responsibility in full self-knowledge of the cultural productions that it increasingly comes to see as its own highest achievement.

In his earlier book *The Logic of the Humanities* (1942), it is once again clear that, again without naming Heidegger, Cassirer sees in the conception of *Dasein*'s thrownness not a new form of humanism but another version of "naturalism, although it speaks the language of a spiritualistic metaphysics."[44] At the same time, *Dasein*'s receptivity to being is linked, in a seeming paradox, to the most extreme epistemological hubris: the voice of being inexplicably bears the inflections of the voice of Heidegger. Oddly, when it does not speak pre-Socratic Greek, it speaks Heideggerian German. Just as the German *Geist* under the Third Reich was indistinguishable from the voice of Hitler, one can hardly avoid asking the question: "Who speaks for being?" One answer is precluded: the question cannot be answered with any objective standard, for such is mere "they" talk, "inauthentic," anonymous chatter, generalities, even if raised to a theoretical precision. Heidegger's ontology inevitably becomes a philosophy of historical success, with Heidegger presiding over the determination of the authentic history of being. If being is the history of being, then the history of being (as determined by . . . Heidegger alone) must be genuine being. Because he rejects verifiable epistemological standards as mere metaphysics, mere willful occlusion of being, Heidegger necessarily ends up with a mystified and oracular presentation of the "voice of being." There is no paradox at all, then. A feigned humility is bound to an actual arrogance. It is to this peculiar and ultimately frightening complex that Cassirer refers when he writes, "This tranquillity and *complete certainty* implies a quietistic principle. The world of culture is no longer seen as a world of free act; it is lived as a fate."[45] Naturalizing human freedom in the name of being, Heidegger is called on, as it were, to become the voice of being. Furthermore, this naturalization of freedom is masked in the hushed tones and cultic robes of romanticism: "For Romanticism," Cassirer writes, "this source of all things spiritual, which is at once manifest and hidden, has its being in the *Spirit of the people* [*Volksgeist*]."[46] Heidegger's ontology, far from being an expression of the truth of being, is no more than *naturalism romantically glossed.* Humanity's freedom is sacrificed on the altar of historical being.

For Cassirer, in contrast, it is neither some mystical *Volkgeist* nor the no less mystifying truth of being but *civilization in its pluralism and universality* that is humanity's *terminus ad quem.* Cassirer interprets civilization more broadly than does Kant not only in terms of reason but more deeply in terms of "symbolic forms," including myth, art, language, and religion as well as science, viewing it as the free achievement of individuals in society. Unlike Sartre's narrow rationalist construction of a for-itself trapped in its own monadic world of meaning or Heidegger's ponderous naturalist ventriloquism, Cassirer's recognition that "man cannot escape from his own achievement" is not confining but rather liberating.[47] The work of civilization is neither solipsist projection nor alienated occlusion of being. Rather, because the human finds its distinctive mark and dignity precisely in creating and living within its own world of symbols, that is, the world of culture, civilization opens up the possibility of self-knowledge. It is in and through civilization, and nowhere else, that humanity can discover and direct what is its own accomplishment. "It is symbolic thought," Cassirer writes, "which overcomes the natural inertia of man and endows him with a new ability, the ability constantly to reshape his human universe."[48] It is thus philosophy, the quest for knowledge guided by universal standards of validity, that offers the opportunity to transform the self-creation of the human into full transparency. Thus the same humanity that creates its world through symbol formation can rise, through self-knowledge, to the high task of taking responsibility for its own self-creation.

It is a foundational principle of Cassirer's humanism that, as *animal symbolicus*, humanity produces and develops its own possibilities in the process of creating the symbolic world of culture. The task of philosophy is not to escape culture by some nostalgic return to "the simple," as Heidegger has called the truth of being, but to transform culture into self-consciousness, to make humanity transparent to itself. "Self-knowledge," Cassirer says in the opening sentence of *An Essay on Man*, "is the highest aim of philosophical knowledge." At the conclusion of that work he writes: "Human culture taken as a whole may be described as the process of man's progressive self-liberation. Language, art, religion, science, are various phases in this process. In all of them man discovers and proves a new power—the power to build up a world of his own, an 'ideal' world. Philosophy cannot give up its search for a fundamental unity in this ideal world. But it does not confound this unity with simplicity."[49] Humanity is cosmopolitan not because it is alienated but precisely because it is cultured, and necessarily so. The personal fate of Heiddegger's thrown *Dasein,* in contrast, submerged in and beholden to the destiny of being, has access neither to verifiable and universally valid truth nor to the ideals of morality and social justice. As early as 1928, after reading Heidegger's *Being and Time,* Cassirer wrote in his (unpublished) notes, contra Heidegger's notion that the everyday public life of *Dasein*—the *Dasein* of culture, social manners, and morals—is no more than "irresolute," "inauthentic," "lost" in the generalities of an interchangeable and essentially anonymous "they-self" (*Mann-selbst*): "We do not understand the general as the mere 'they,' but as '*objective* mind and objective *culture.*' Such objectivity remains for Heidegger inaccessible to the mind. . . . The 'impersonal' does not consist merely in the pale, diluted social form of the average, the everydayness of the 'they,' but in the form of *trans*-personal meaning. For this trans-personal Heidegger's philosophy has no access."[50]

For Cassirer, humanity—if there is to be a humanity, a community of humans—cannot be divorced from the essential idealism that lies in the objective or transpersonal character of its symbolic world as such, whether mythic, artistic, linguistic, religious, or scientific. The unity of humankind lies not in a childlike and irresponsible subjection to being, to the mesmerizing philosophical or political leader, but rather in the unity of the symbol-forming function itself, the essential *communicability*—the transpersonal meaning—of culture and cultures as symbol formations. Far from occluding the genuinely human, as Heidegger would have us believe, culture is precisely the expression and the path—through self-knowledge—of "man's progressive self-liberation." This is Cassirer's humanist philosophy of culture and his radical criticism of what he understood to be the profoundly arrogant, irresponsible, and merely romantic naturalism of Heidegger's "fundamental ontology," if not also—although Cassirer, intellectual gentleman to the end, nowhere says this—of Heidegger the man.

Levinas: *Humanism of the Other*

Where does Levinas stand in relation to this concatenation of conflicting ideas and worldviews regarding humanism, freedom, culture, and being—in relation, that is, to Sartre, Heidegger, and Cassirer? What is humanism for Levinas? What is the positive and critical import of his humanism of the other?

Levinas's own philosophy—"ethical metaphysics," as Edith Wyschogrod has aptly labeled it—was developed over many decades. It began to take shape in hints and suggestions found in early expository and critical studies of Husserl's phenomenology and Heidegger's ontology published in the 1930s. It took its earliest positive form in the mid-1940s, in the "existentialist" atmosphere of postwar Paris, in two short books: *Existence and Existents* and *Time and the Other*,[51] both appearing in 1947. It appeared finally in its most articulate and mature form in two masterworks: *Totality and Infinity* and *Otherwise than Being or Beyond Essence*. The central chapters of the latter work were written and published as separate articles in 1967 and 1968, a few years before the three essays gathered in *Humanism of the Other* were published. Levinas's reflections on humanism, therefore, appear at the time of, and represent, the full height and maturation of his thought. Levinas's humanism of the other is a philosophy engaged at close quarters with the philosophical debates of the time and place, caught up in a reflection on the events of May 1968, the then current intellectual Parisian vogue of structuralism, French readings of Hegel and Nietzsche, and most particularly the French fascination with Heideggerian ontology. But it is also the very core of Levinas's thought as a whole and his unique contribution to Western philosophy. From beginning to end Levinas's thought is a humanism of the other.

The distinctive moment of Levinas's philosophy transcends its articulation but is nevertheless not difficult to discern: *the superlative moral priority of the other person*. It proposes a conception of the "humanity of the human," the "subjectivity of the subject," according to which being "for-the-other" takes precedence over, is better than, being for-itself. Ethics conceived as a metaphysical anthropology is therefore nothing less than "first philosophy." The positive moment of Levinas's thought thus lies in the moral transcendence of the other person. Concomitantly, it lies in moral response to transcendence, a self charged with taking responsibility for the other. The former, the transcendence of the other, is the central topic of *Totality and Infinity*. The latter, the responsible self, is the central topic of *Otherwise than Being*. Of course, transcendence and responsibility are inseparable moments of concrete ethical encounter, the face-to-face of the self and other. The "otherness" of the other person arises precisely as the moral imperative that pierces the self with moral obligation, with service to the other. Indeed, the true selfhood of the self occurs precisely in and as this service. One is not called on to "love thy neighbor *as* oneself," according to the biblical precept, as if self-love preceded other-love and were the measure of other-love. Rather, the proper formulation of Levinas's thought is more extreme, an infinite demand never satisfied even in its fulfillment: to "love thy neighbor *is* oneself." The moral self is the self-emptying, the "fission," the "denucleation," of selfhood in and as responsibility for the other—up to the ultimate self-sacrifice, to die for the other's welfare. Care for the other trumps care for the self, *is* care for the self. Nothing is more significant.

The critical moment of Levinas's thought follows from its uncompromising start in the radical imperatives of ethical service, in an unremitting critique of all the more or less subtle circuits of self-love, self-satisfaction, and self-relation. In those circuits, however serene or strenuous, however abstract or existential, including the whole of being or culture, the subject complacently returns to itself, overlooking, ignoring, neglecting, abandoning, escaping, and otherwise refusing the priority of its moral responsibility to and for the other person. Under the inexorable imperative of the other, the pure but inescapably immanent activity of Sartre's for-itself, Heidegger's conception of *Dasein* beholden to the historical revelations of being, and Cassirer's transcendental attachment to culture are all to be criticized for missing the priority of the *moral transcendence that ultimately gives significance* to human freedom in all its varied cultural and historical manifestations.

A humanism of the other is the heart of Levinas's philosophy, not merely an occasional topic of the hour or day, one of the many ephemeral Parisian intellectual fashions. For Levinas, the dignity of the self arises in and as an unsurpassable moral responsibility to and for the other person. And moral responsibility for the one who faces leads to the demand for justice for all those who do not face, for all others, all humanity. They too have the right to moral relations. Justice derives not from the state, which must nonetheless institute and maintain justice, but from the transcendence of the other person, the "widow, the orphan, the stranger." It is in relation to this irreducible and immediate responsibility that, in the name of justice, culture, history, organized religion, the state, science, and philosophy take on their ultimate senses and have their ultimate justifications. The entire realm of the universal, in all its particular historically determined manifestations, emerges from and is guided by the imperatives of morality and is subject therefore to moral judgment.

For Levinas as for Cassirer, philosophy is ineluctably anthropological without being relativist. For Levinas, however, the absolute standard of philosophical anthropology derives first from its ethical height rather than its epistemological scruples. Thus Levinas, again like Cassirer before him and for many of the same reasons, rejects the legerdemain of the anti-humanist naturalism that drives Heideggerian ontology. Transcendence is the moral surplus of the other person, not the generosity of being. In the name of moral transcendence, Levinas rejects Cassirer's adherence to culture and a philosophy of culture as the source of meaning. These, then, are the broad lines of Levinas's ethical metaphysics.

Signification and Sense

A critique of Heidegger is found on almost every page of Levinas's philosophical writings. Heidegger is his preeminent antagonist. In contrast, Cassirer's name never appears anywhere in his works, not even once. So, too, Levinas rarely uses the term *symbol,* preferring terms such as *signifier, sign, signification, significance, meaning, saying, said,* and *expression* when speaking of language. What is the meaning of this silence, this suppression? Certainly Levinas is no Cassirerian or, for that matter, neo-Kantian. It is clear that he finds the philosophy of culture, as he finds Kant, neo-Kantianism, and Husserl as well, inadequate because of their overriding epistemological predispositions. Nevertheless, when in the name of justice Levinas returns to the level of the universal, to the manifestation of being, the appropriate philosophical supplement to his thought is Cassirer's nuanced philosophy of culture, stripped of its philosophical self-interpretation. Could it be this proximity, so different from that of 1929, that accounts for Levinas's silence?

Whatever the answer to this question, and whatever the validity of the claim that the philosophy of culture is the perfect supplement to an ethical metaphysics, in "Signification and Sense" Levinas finally comes to grips with Cassirer. Here, as in most of Levinas's philosophical writings, the topic is the origin and nature of meaning. Such is usually the central topic of contemporary continental or phenomenological philosophy. More specifically, however, the question of meaning in "Signification and Sense" is raised in relation to cultural meaning and symbols.

Early in the chapter there is an oblique but nonetheless unmistakable allusion to the Cassirer-Heidegger debate when Levinas employs, as if casually, the expressions *terminus a quo* and *terminus ad quem*.[52] He mentions neither Cassirer nor Davos, but the hint is clear enough. Referring to Merleau-Ponty rather than to Cassirer, however, Levinas begins the chapter acknowledging that all contemporary theories of meaning are grounded in the recognition of the integral unity of meaning and sense, sign and signifier. "The anti-Platonism of contemporary philosophy," he writes, "lies in the subordination of intellect to expression."[53] Truth is not a matter of abstracting away from the particularities of language and history to a pure realm of forms or concepts. Symbols, language, culture, and the sense of signification are indeed—as Cassirer would certainly be the first to agree—the home of meaning, no longer to be reduced away as obstructions to an ideal intellectual order. "Cultures," Levinas observes, "are no longer obstacles that separate us from the essential and the intelligible; they are the paths by which we can reach it."[54] In the philosophical search for the nature and origin of meaning, this new appreciation for the positive role of symbols, cultures, and history arises because "signification is not separate from the access leading to it. *Access is part of signification itself.* The scaffoldings are never dismantled. The ladder is never drawn up."[55] In earlier writings Levinas had attributed this insight to Husserl. It was already central to Bergson. In any event, both Heidegger and Cassirer, as contemporary philosophers, also adhere to this general outlook, even if Cassirer takes the integral unity of expressive language, the symbol, to reside in culture, whereas Heidegger takes it to be a function of the epochal and oracular "truth" given by being. Significantly, Levinas sides

with Cassirer against Heidegger. For instance, consider Heidegger's repeated insistence (the "voice of being") that the ontological significance
of the contemporary epoch is "technological," that the all-pervading
character of the present epoch is determined by *technē* and the technological occlusion of being's future revelations. For Levinas, however,
"the technical designation of the universe is itself a modality of culture."[56] Culture, as Cassirer taught, is the realm of signification; the
"truth of being," in any event, must be understood in terms of culture
and not vice verse.

For Levinas, however, meaning as expression—signification bound
to sense and hence to cultural symbols—originates neither in being nor
in culture. Significance originally emerges from the face-to-face encounter as an ethical event, that is, from the other person as moral command and the self as moral response. "In other words, before it is a
celebration of being, expression is a relation with the one to whom I express the expression and whose presence is already required so that my
cultural gesture of expression can be produced."[57] I am distinguishing
between the significance and the signification of expression. This follows the distinction, highlighted in *Otherwise than Being*, between what
is said (*le Dit*), the contents of discourse, which are certainly cultural
expressions, and the more original and interhuman saying (*le Dire*) of
them, which is an ethical event. Expression is not absorbed into an ontological dialectic of revelation and concealment, à la Heidegger, but
neither is expression sufficiently grasped by greater self-knowledge regarding lateral reference to its broader cultural context and the transcendental conditions of that cultural context, à la Cassirer. Rather, the
expression of the other, what Levinas calls the "face" (*visage*), as origi-
nating in the unreachable and nonthematizable transcendence of the
other—beyond being and "before culture"[58]—puts the self into question, moral question. The other disturbs, upsets, and overwhelms the
self-relation of the self with a moral obligation to respond that cuts
deeper—is more important—than cultural formations or the ontological configuration of being. Whether the other's persona is that of a
self-styled spokesperson for being or of a cultured cosmopolitan, the
very otherness of the other—that which constitutes the other's humanity—is originally encountered across moral imperative. The ethi-

cal event of intersubjectivity is thus achieved via the "deformalization," to use another of Levinas's terms from *Otherwise than Being,* of the other and the self. Symbolic forms are interrupted, overcharged, and broken by moral imperatives. Symbols cannot "contain" the moral imperatives that ultimately drive them and give them sense. "Thou shall not kill," for instance, is first an immediate command—the very face of the other— before it is a proposition, inscription, or sign. The spirit of the oral Torah paradoxically precedes and gives sense to the words of the written Torah, breathing life into it.

Because he stands on the side of a metaphysical anthropology and humanism against ontology, Levinas must therefore clarify his philosophical differences vis-à-vis Cassirer. "What is at stake here," Levinas writes, contra the unnamed Cassirer (and Sartre), "is the calling of consciousness into question, and not a consciousness of a calling into question."[59] Ethical transcendence ruptures the syntheses that define consciousness, including the self-possession of its "symbol-forming" function. Moral vigilance, readiness, or wakefulness precedes and undermines the slumber of self-consciousness. "The nudity of the face," Levinas writes, "is a stripping with no cultural ornament—an absolution—a detachment of its form in the heart of production of form."[60] Moral obligation effects a deformalization more pressing, more immediate, than the immediacy of self-awareness. "But this coming from *elsewhere* is not a *symbolic reference* to this *elsewhere* as to a term."[61] Morality short-circuits the symbol-forming function of consciousness. The significance of signification is first and emphatically moral.

Thus, precisely because it overlooks the priority of ethical deformalization, Cassirer's philosophy of culture inevitably falls into the very cultural relativism of which it accused Heidegger. It loses its capacity of moral judgment, which is vital to any humanism, and thus to Levinas. Regarding the unwonted relativism inherent in Cassirer's deference to culture, Levinas writes: "It is extremely important to stress the anteriority of sense with regard to cultural signs. To attach all signification to culture, making no distinction between signification and cultural expression, between signification and the art that prolongs cultural expression, is to recognize that all cultural personalities realize the mind by the same rights. Then no signification could be detached from those countless cultures that would allow us to make judgments on them."[62] Before cultural expression, before the said, lies the universal but deformalized humanism of the other, the saying of the other as other, as another human being. This is not simply before as an epistemological condition but rather before as better, as unconditional ethical imperative. The first significance, the significance of signification, is imposed in the irreducibly immediate and imperative deformalization effected by the moral imposition of the other, in the "trauma" of obligation and responsibility to respond, in ethical proximity. Signification is bound to sense, to cultural expressions, to be sure, but more originally it is driven and uplifted by ethical significance, beyond being and before culture. Hence it is here, and not within culture, that one discovers the source of cultural expression as social activity and the unsettling ground from which one can judge—ethically in terms of goodness and not merely epistemologically in terms of validity—the world of culture within which humans necessarily live.

In the chapter entitled "Without Identity" Levinas turns to his primary antagonist, Heidegger. I will take a short and selective look at this chapter less to review Levinas's criticisms of Heidegger, whom Levinas considers elsewhere more broadly and deeply, than to show the extent to which these criticisms reproduce Cassirer's earlier rejection of Heidegger before and after the Davos debate.

In the second subsection of "Without Identity," entitled simply "Heidegger," Levinas writes the following of both structuralism and Heidegger: "The social sciences and Heidegger lead to the triumph of mathematical intelligibility, sending the subject, the individual, his unicity and election, back into ideology, or else rooting man in being, making him its messenger and poet."[63] As a humanist, Levinas rejects any interpretation of the human, structuralist or ontological, that reduces the human to the inhuman—in Heidegger's case, to the notion that *Dasein* is enrooted or thrown into being. Following Cassirer, Levinas sees a latent and reductive naturalism in Heidegger's conception of thrown *Dasein*: "The ecstasy of intentionality would then be founded in the truth of being, in parousia. Didn't naturalism foresee this mode of foundation by posing consciousness as an avatar of nature?"[64] Despite his keen phenomenological appreciation for the expressive character of meaning, for human embodiment, and for the relevance of history, Heidegger never sufficiently grasped the irreducible significance—for Levinas, the ethical significance—of the human.

Furthermore, despite his admiration for *Being and Time*, Levinas not only challenged its fundamental posture, the ontological reversal it prepares, but, over the course of his own intellectual development, eventually rejected and provided alternative accounts—as is appropriate in the science of phenomenology—of Heidegger's particular phenomenological analyses. For instance, Levinas does not view embodiment as taking on its finality from the "ownmost" (*eigenlich*) character or individuating "mineness" (*Jemeinigkeit*) of being-toward-death, as Heidegger thought. Rather, Levinas takes the key to embodiment to lie in its vulnerability, a vulnerability that opens the human to the suffering of others. "The humanity of man, subjectivity, is a responsibility for others, an extreme vulnerability."[65] One is moved to alleviate the pain of others because as an embodied being, the self enjoys the elements, is happy through them, and is thereby also able to appreciate viscerally the pain of physical suffering, deprivation, disease, and aging in others. One does not simply live in the resoluteness of one's own mortal being, released to the larger revelatory identity of epochal being. Rather, in a moral vulnerability to the other's vulnerabilities, suffering for the other's suffering, man lives for a future beyond his own death, whether in the immediacy of the face of the other person whose needs are one's responsibilities—"unto death," if need be—or in consideration of an unredeemed humanity and its future generations, for whom one is bound by the demands of justice.

Embodiment, for Levinas, is not the inevitable closure of the mortality of each; rather, it is openness to the mortality of others. Suffering and dying are not private affairs but solicit the concern of the human community, calling for aid and compassion from physicians, parents, siblings, children, science, hospitals, philanthropic generosity, and so on. Suffering and mortality, then, are first and foremost the suffering and mortality of the other, from whom one's own suffering, otherwise useless, takes on meaning. The significance of embodiment is neither attachment to self nor attachment to being but rather vulnerability to the other, hence moral compassion, "suffering for the suffering of the other."[66] Nor can such an account of suffering be confused with a quietist pietism, the vicarious but private martyrdom of the beautiful soul. To suffer for others is to serve them: to provide for their concrete material needs for nourishment, clothing, health, shelter, and employment; to assuage their pains, anxieties, and fears; to respect their freedom and dignity; to care for the other's requirements before protecting or catering to one's own various social identities. Levinas is fond of quoting Rabbi Israel Salanter, the nineteenth-century Eastern European rabbi known for his zealous commitment to ethical self-examination and self-improvement: "The other's material needs are my spiritual needs." The first body is the body of the other, from whom my own embodiment—in its blend of passivity and activity—takes on its significance as moral compassion.

The so-called law of nature, in contrast, is self-preservation, whether through inertia (homeostasis, equilibrium) or aggrandizement (will to power). Being takes care of itself; such is its very essence—*conatus essendi,* to "persevere in being." From the perspective of nature, as Spinoza taught, pleasure, which ignorant humans call "good," is whatever increases one's own power, and pain, which ignorant humans call "evil," is whatever decreases one's own power. Such would be the truth of being, envisioned without human prejudice, *ethica ordine geometrico demonstrata.* But for a genuine humanism, being is not the be all and end all. "To be or not to be," Levinas comments, "is that the question? Is it not rather one's right to be?" To be human is to care for the other above oneself, to overcome the natural indifference and countercurrent of being in nonindifference and compassion toward the other—the "wisdom of love." It is a painful wisdom, "a skin turned inside out," to use Levinas's striking phrase, providing for the other the food one would enjoy eating, the clothing one would enjoy wearing, the money one would enjoy spending. Humanity is constituted in the moral overcoming of the natural reflexivity of being, its recurrence, its selfishness. In contrast to *Homo sapiens,* the first word addressed to man—*Adam*—is a moral command. Because the human self is embodied and hence enjoys the elements, to care for the other's enjoyment becomes a visceral concern of the self, its moral obligation. Concerned for the concerns of the other, to be for the other before being for oneself is one's true self—without external identity and without internal identity—the self that rises to the height of its proper humanity, its proper dignity.

Conclusion

Contra Heidegger, Cassirer correctly locates the origin of meaning within the human dimension—indeed, contra Sartre, within the social.[67] So, for instance, Heidegger's grandiose assertion that the modern epoch is dominated by technology even if the "essence" of technology is not technological, remains inextricably a cultural rather than an ontological determination. For Levinas, of course, to locate the origin of meaning in the human dimension means that its source lies in the irreducible and unsurpassable moral obligation to respond to the other person.

Contra Cassirer, Heidegger correctly asserts that meaning must be understood in terms of a greater transcendence than that allowed by an interpretation of the human as bound to culture, to symbol formation and self-knowledge, which Levinas has called the said. Such a view ends up caught in the morass of cultural relativism and thus is rendered incapable of the universal moral judgment that Cassirer intended to defend and that Levinas does defend in the name of justice. Despite its inescapable cultural manifestation as the said, meaning as saying transcends culture.

Contra Heidegger, however, the transcendence of meaning is lost when sacrificed on the altar of being. Levinas adopts Cassirer's critique of Heidegger that fundamental ontology is but another avatar of naturalism. Neither Levinas nor Cassirer envisions the human dimension as thrown or enrooted like a plant in the ground of being, bending to the presence and absence of its light. For neither thinker is human finitude puppetlike, even if performing in the vast theater of being or characterized by the dependence of a ventriloquist's dummy on the lap of being, mouthing the words spoken by being. Rejecting Cassirer's fidelity to culture, however, Levinas views the transcendence of meaning as transcending cultural determination. The transcendence of meaning—and human dignity—derives from the absolute moral priority of the other person, that is to say, from the humanism of the other. Before it is a function of being or enmeshed in culture, the significance of signification lies in saying, in the excellence of moral responsibility and obligation. To be for the other otherwise than being and before culture, to serve the other morally, and to serve all others in justice—here lies the ultimate exigency of meaning and the dignity of humankind.

We can now see why the mature Levinas so regretted his part in the farcical play at Davos in 1929, why more than forty years later he still sought pardon from Mrs. Cassirer. It was Cassirer, after all, who consistently and with much personal travail and courage defended the noble ethics of humanism. He did so both in his life and—through the disinterested passion of scholarship—in his prodigious intellectual output. "To act for distant things," Levinas writes, "at a time when Hitlerism triumphed, in the deaf hours of that night without hours, to act independently of any evaluation of the 'forces in presence,' was undoubtedly the height of nobility."[68]

He felt regret and sought pardon, too, because as a young man Levinas had mocked Cassirer in a debate with *Martin Heidegger:* Heidegger, who in that darkening time and then in the deaf hours of the night that followed saw fit to oppose humanism. Heidegger, who in his life and thought, grandiose self-interpretations notwithstanding, collaborated with the murderous regime of the Nazis. (It was Heidegger, not Cassirer, who then and thereafter sided with "anti-Semitism" both in its specific sense of hatred of Jews and in the broader sense Levinas gave to this term: "the same hatred of the other, the same anti-Semitism"). Heidegger, who saw fit neither to apologize for his membership in the Nazi Party nor, in his prolific postwar years, to even mention, let alone to think, the vast and terrible horror of the Holocaust; the *Seinsfrage,* for all its alleged depth, was somehow blind to such events, such inessentials, mere "ontic" affairs. Is it any wonder, then, that Levinas was haunted with regret and sought pardon for what under almost any other circumstances would surely have been a long forgotten youthful folly?

Levinas's relation to Cassirer is not simply a matter of psychological interest. It has profound philosophical implications, especially for a proper conception of humanism and its responsibilities. To see Levinas's humanism in the context of the Cassirer-Heidegger debate is to free his thought from the facile attempts, often so clever—one thinks of Derrida especially—to link his ethical metaphysics, by an ingenious dialectical violation, to the very ontology he radically opposed. According to this line of thinking, Heidegger would be Levinas's accomplice by opposition, his tar baby. The narcissism and allied hubris of this type of approach are already evident in Heidegger's usurpation of Kant. And such an allergic reading has already been perpetrated on Levinas's writings, as if in criticizing Heidegger, the "violence" of Levinas's thought must turn against him. Surely, however, there is a vast difference between the insight of philosophical criticism and the blindness of self-serving appropriation.[69] Let us ask, does Levinas inevitably return to Heidegger when in the name of justice he returns from metaphysics to being, from the other person to all of humanity?

Not at all. Precisely here we see Levinas's deeper relation and deepest debt to Cassirer. When Levinas returns to being from the metaphysics of the other, he does so in the name of a call to universal justice, _tikkun olam,_ to "repair the world," a call that is never removed from—indeed, is guided by—the responsibilities of moral proximity. The world of being to which he returns and—because there is nothing mystical about Levinas's thought—that he has never left is Cassirer's world of culture, the world of symbols, the said. The world of culture receives its ultimate sense from the moral transcendence of the other, to be sure, but it is precisely the world of culture that is so valued, charged with responsibilities from the moral to the juridical. Contra a perverse and sophistical dialectic that would revive what one opposes in the very opposition, Levinas, like Cassirer, radically contests the mystified and mystifying irresponsibility of a participatory submergence of the human in the inhuman, whether in the name of being or in an even more tenuous semiotic play of language. In such opposition there is no lapse back into the ponderous anonymity of fundamental ontology or the meandering vagaries of equivocation, no childish surrender, no compromise with evil.

Responsibilities are infinite, even if humans are insufficient for them. Rather guilt than guile, rather responsibility than risibility. The call to justice is a high task, even if—and especially because—the road is long and the outcome unsure. In the words of Rabbi Tarfon, from Pirke Avot: "It is not incumbent upon you to complete the work; yet, you are not free to desist from it."[70]

About the Translation

Nidra Poller is the first to translate Levinas's *Humanism of the Other* as a book. Alphonso Lingis—the translator of three of Levinas's four most important philosophical works, *Existence and Existents, Totality and Infinity,* and *Otherwise than Being or Beyond Essence* (the fourth is *Time and the Other,* which I had the privilege to translate)—has previously translated the three chapters that make up *Humanism of the Other.* They appear as separate chapters in a collection Lingis translated, edited, and entitled *Collected Philosophical Papers.* I will not say that one translator has gotten Levinas right and the other has gotten him wrong. Both are good translations. What then is the difference? It seems to me—and perhaps this is only a matter of taste—that Poller's translation has a smoother flow, is more in tune with literary nuances, without sacrificing the philosophical precision of Levinas's meaning.

Let the reader beware: Levinas does not read easily either in the original French or in translation. There is a virtue in this, however. When years ago I was worried about the awkwardness of my translation of Levinas's seminal article "God and Philosophy," Bob Lechner, then editor of *Philosophy Today,* where the translation was first published, soothed my anxieties by remarking: "One does not read Levinas, one meditates on him." I think his comment is both true and instructive. Anyone who has seriously read Levinas's philosophical writings cannot but be aware of their depth and originality. Almost every sentence includes one or several allusions to other philosophers and thinkers. They are writings thoroughly grounded in and responsive to the entire history of the West. In this sense they are "master" writings.

In certain instances Poller improves or provides a fruitful alternative to the Lingis translation. For example, Lingis translates one remark in the fourth subsection of "Humanism and An-Archy" as follows: "The exteriority of the alliance is maintained in the effort required by the responsibility for others"; Poller, however, translates the same passage thus: "The exteriority of the covenant is maintained precisely in the effort demanded by responsibility for others." The French reads: "Cette extériorité de l'alliance se maintient précisément dans l'effort qu'exige la responsabilité pour les autres." Should Levinas's *l'alliance* be translated "alliance," as in Lingis, or "covenant," as in Poller? In this instance it seems to me that Poller's choice is more sensitive to the religious—especially Jewish—rather than the political-military connotation of Levinas's usage.

Along similar lines, in the fifth subsection of "Signification and Sense," Levinas concludes a sentence with the clause "la symphonie où tous les sens deviennent chantants, le cantique des cantiques." Lingis translates this as "the symphony in which all the meanings can sing, canticle of canticles" (in a footnote Adriaan Peperzak adds, "Allusion to the *Song of Songs* of Solomon"). Poller translates it thus: "the symphony where all senses become song, the song of songs." Is Levinas's *les sens* Lingis's "meanings" or Poller's "senses"? It is a difficult question. Poller's choice retains a certain ambiguity but succeeds in linking the term to the title of the article, "Signification and Sense" (*La Signification et le sens*). Lingis, however, translated the title of Levinas's article as "Sense and Meaning," so that consistency forces him to translate *les sens* as "the meanings." But I want to draw attention to another matter. Is *le cantique des cantiques* better rendered by Lingis's "canticle of canticles," which preserves the Vulgate Bible's rendition of "Song of Songs" (as the Peperzak footnote indicates) or by Poller's straightforwardly biblical rendering: "song of songs." Again this presents a difficult question, a matter of sensitivity to different traditions. Poller's repeated use of *song* has the virtue of linking *chantants* to its etymological relative *cantiques,* but Lingis's translation retains a link to Levinas's later reference in the same chapter to Paul Valéry's "Canticle of the Columns." An agonizing choice for any translator! In this instance I think it is better that we have *both* translations.

In one case in the same chapter, however, Lingis simply blunders—and one must wonder why—and Poller gets it right. Levinas writes: "Elle se dessine en dehors de la 'délectation morose' de l'échec et des consolations par lesquelles Nietzsche définit le christianisme." Lingis translates this as follows: "It takes form outside of the morose savoring of failures and consolations, which for Nietzsche defines religion." Poller translates it thus: "It is traced outside the 'morose delectation' in failure and consolations by which Nietzsche defines Christianity." Poller's version is superior to Lingis's because Lingis (regardless of what one thinks about *savoring* versus *delectation*) deletes Levinas's quotation marks. Also, Lingis uses the plural *failures* when in the French original and in Poller it is singular. But these are trivial compared to what follows. Why Lingis translates Levinas's *christianisme* by "religion," when Poller's "Christianity" is of course the correct translation, is hard to fathom. Perhaps an oversight? Perhaps a theological agenda?

But I do not mean to nitpick. One can always learn French. Just as I think Lingis's herculean labors as a translator have served Levinas's English-speaking readers well, so too Nidra Poller's new and first complete translation of *Humanism of the Other* is a very welcome addition to the English-language versions of the works of Emmanuel Levinas. Translation is a thankless labor. The best translators aim for their own invisibility, "without identity," placing the other before the self, letting the author's text "speak" for itself. This is something Heidegger failed to grasp and something Levinas and Cassirer understood very well. In this service Poller has succeeded, and for this let us be thankful.

Notes

1. Ernst Cassirer, *The Philosophy of Symbolic Forms,* 3 vols., trans. Ralph Manheim (New Haven, Conn.: Yale University Press, 1955–57): vol. 1, *Language* (1955); vol. 2, *Mythical Thought* (1955); vol. 3, *The Phenomenology of Knowledge* (1957).

2. Ernst Cassirer, *An Essay on Man* (New Haven, Conn.: Yale University Press, 1944).

3. Martin Heidegger, *Being and Time,* trans. John Macquarrie and Edward Robinson (New York: Harper and Row, 1962); idem, trans. Joan Stambaugh (Albany: State University of New York Press, 1966).

4. Martin Heidegger, "Letter on Humanism," trans. William Barrett and Henry D. Aiken, in *The Existentialist Tradition,* ed. Nino Langiulli (Garden City, N.Y.: Doubleday, 1971), 204–45.

5. Emmanuel Levinas, "La Signification et le sens," *Revue de Métaphysique et de Morale* 69, no. 2 (April–June 1964): 256–66.

6. Emmanuel Levinas, "Humanisme et an-archie," *Revue Internationale de Philosophie* 85–86, nos. 3–4 (1968): 323–37.

7. Emmanuel Levinas, "Sans indentité," *L'Éphémère* 13 (1970): 27–44. The three articles constituting *The Humanism of the Other* appear in a collection of articles by Levinas translated and edited by Alphonso Lingis: Emmanuel Levinas, *Collected Philosophical Papers* (The Hague: Martinus Nijhoff, 1987).

8. Emmanuel Levinas, *Humanisme de l'autre homme* (Montpellier: Fata Morgana, 1972).

9. Emmanuel Levinas, *Otherwise than Being or Beyond Essence,* trans. Alphonso Lingis (The Hague: Martinus Nijhoff, 1981).

10. Emmanuel Levinas, *Totality and Infinity,* trans. Alphonso Lingis (The Hague: Martinus Nijhoff, 1978).

11. This volume, 48.

12. Immanuel Kant, *Werke: Gesamtausgabe in 10 Bänden und einen Erganzungsband,* ed. Ernst Cassirer (Berlin: Bruno Cassirer, 1912). Cassirer edited vols. 4 and 6 and, with Artur Buchenau, coedited vols. 9 and 10.

13. Ernst Cassirer, *Kant's Life and Thought,* trans. James Haden (New Haven, Conn.: Yale University Press, 1981).

14. Martin Heidegger, *Kant and the Problem of Metaphysics,* trans. James S. Churchill (Bloomington: Indiana University Press, 1962). The book's appendixes also contain the "protocols" of the Cassirer-Heidegger debate at Davos, as well as Heidegger's review of volumes 1 and 2 of Cassirer's *Philosophy of Symbolic Forms.*

15. Ernst Cassirer, "*Kant and the Problem of Metaphysics,*" trans. Moltke S. Gram, in *Kant: Disputed Questions,* ed. Moltke S. Gram (Chicago: Quadrangle Books, 1967), 131–57.

16. The most complete account of the Davos encounter is to be found in Ernst Cassirer and Martin Heidegger, *Débat sur le Kantisme et la philosophie,* ed. Pierre Aubenque (Paris: Éditions Beauchesne, 1972).

17. *Dasein* is, of course, Heidegger's term for human subjectivity. It is a conventional German word meaning "existence" and literally translates as "there" (da) "being" (*sein*), or "being-there." Heidegger uses it to avoid the subjectivist implications of the terms *subject* and *subjectivity,* which hark back to the Cartesian notion of the self as an enclosed self-reflection or consciousness. As I will discuss, Heidegger employs this term to mark a more contemporary notion of the self as always engaged in and with the world, always transcending itself into the world, hence "ecstatic."

18. Cassirer and Heidegger, *Débat,* 74 (my translation). In 1934, just four years after the Davos debate, Levinas published "Phenomenology," a review of several books, where, apropos of a volume by one of Heidegger's disciples, he wrote:

"One cannot deny the interest of attempts like those of Heidegger and Mörchen. Fustel de Coulanges said with contempt that to philosophize is to think whatever one wants. So that to philosophize is also to make others say whatever pleases us. In the face of the talent deployed by Heidegger, the contempt is perhaps a bit much. But he is imprecise—whatever the philosophy of history one professes—to entitle this new genre of studies the 'history of philosophy.' They cannot replace the scholarship in which we confide under this title in France by mistrusting [*méfiant*]—according to the word of Delbos—those enterprises that, under the pretext of discovering the profound meaning of a philosophy, commence by disregarding its meaning" (Emmanuel Levinas, "Phénoménologie," *Revue Philosophique de la France et de l'Étranger* 118, no. 12 [1934]: 414–20). I thank Georges Hansel for bringing this citation to my attention.

19. In its own way, within the context of contemporary or existential thought, this dispute reproduces the earlier dispute between Friedrich Albert Lange, who in his monumental *History of Materialism* (1866) had interpreted Kant psychologically, and Lange's successor at the University of Marburg and Cassirer's teacher, Hermann Cohen, who in the early 1870s interpreted Kant idealistically. Even more broadly, the Cassirer-Heidegger debate over both Kant and humanism recalls the debate between Luther, for whom salvation came to the faithful entirely from the free grace of God, and Erasmus, for whom human responsibility and moral integrity contributed to salvation as well.

20. Cassirer, *Essay on Man,* 1.

21. Ibid.

22. Emmanuel Levinas, *Les Imprévus de l'histoire,* ed. Pierre Hayat (Montpellier: Fata Morgana, 1994), 209 (my translation). This passage appears just after Levinas discusses the Nazis and Heidegger's anti-humanism. Levinas observes that "the absence of care (*souci*) for the other in Heidegger and his personal political adventure are linked." An English translation of *Les Imprévus de l'histoire* is forthcoming from the University of Illinois Press.

23. Ibid., 209–10.

24. See François Poirié, *Emmanuel Levinas: Qui êtes-vous?* (Lyon: La Manufacture, 1987), 76–78. In the interview with Poirié, Levinas gives a longer and more detailed account of the 1929 Davos encounter.

25. Ibid., 78: "Et je m'en suis beaucoup voulu pendant les années hitleriennes d'avoir préféré Heidegger à Davos."

26. Ernst Cassirer, *Logic of the Humanities,* trans. Clarence Smith Howe (New Haven, Conn.: Yale University Press, 1960).

27. Ernst Cassirer, *The Myth of the State,* ed. Charles W. Hendel (New Haven, Conn.: Yale University Press, 1946).

28. Jean-Paul Sartre, *The Transcendence of the Ego: An Existential Theory of Consciousness,* trans. Forrest Williams and Robert Kirkpatrick (New York: Farrar, Straus and Giroux, 1957).

29. Jean-Paul Sartre, *Being and Nothingness: An Essay on Phenomenological Ontology,* trans. Hazel E. Barnes (New York: Washington Square, 1966).

30. Jean-Paul Sartre, "Existentialism Is a Humanism," trans. Philip Mairet, in *The Existentialist Tradition,* ed. Nino Langiulli (Garden City, N.Y.: Doubleday, 1971), 395.

31. Ibid., 396.

32. Ibid., 399.

33. Heidegger, "Letter," 217.

34. Ibid., 216.

35. Ibid., 215.

36. Ibid., 208, 209.

37. Ibid., 221.

38. Ibid., 218.

39. Ibid., 220.

40. Ibid., 227.

41. Ibid., 229 (emphasis added).

42. Levinas, *Myth of the State,* 293.

43. Cassirer, *Essay on Man,* 18.

44. Heidegger, "Letter," 7–8.

45. Ibid., 8 (emphasis added).

46. Ibid., 7.

47. Cassirer, *Essay on Man,* 25.

48. Ibid., 62.

49. Ibid., 1, 228.

50. Ernst Cassirer, "'Mind' and 'Life': Heidegger (an Unpublished Manuscript)," trans. John Michael Krois, *Philosophy and Rhetoric* 16, no. 3 (1983): 161.

51. Emmanuel Levinas, *Existence and Existents,* trans. Alphonso Lingis (The Hague: Martinus Nijhoff, 1978). A more accurate translation of the French title, *De l'existence à l'existant,* might have been *From Existence to the Existent.* Emmanuel Levinas, *Time and the Other (and Additional Essays),* trans. Richard A. Cohen (Pittsburgh, Pa.: Duquesne University Press, 1987).

52. This volume, 10.

53. This volume, 19.

54. This volume, 18.

55. This volume, 20.

56. This volume, 21.

57. This volume, 30.

58. This volume, 36. "Before Culture" is the name Levinas gives to subsection 8 of this chapter.

59. Levinas, *Collected Papers*, 97. Here I prefer the Lingis translation. Levinas writes: "Il s'agit de la mise en question de la conscience et non pas d'une conscience de la mise en question." Poller has translated this as follows: "This is a challenge of consciousness, not a consciousness of the challenge" (this volume, 33).

60. This volume, 32.

61. This volume, 39.

62. This volume, 36.

63. This volume, 61.

64. This volume, 63.

65. This volume, 67.

66. This volume, 63.

67. Locating the source of meaning in the human is precisely what Levinas always praised in the "dialogical" philosophy of Martin Buber, which is often—erroneously—confused with Levinas's ethical metaphysics of the face-to-face. Buber must also be given credit, along with Cassirer, for being one of the earliest and sharpest critics of Heidegger's ontology. Levinas, nonetheless, is no less sharp a critic of Buber's account of sociality as an "I-thou" encounter.

68. This volume, 29.

69. See note 18, where Levinas pointedly distinguishes between the methods of the "history of philosophy" and the interpretive violence of appropriation.

70. Mishna Pirke Avot, chapter 2, mishnah 16.

Translator's Note

The fact is that English offers no equivalent to the *se* that so deftly slips a French verb into the reflexive. In most circumstances "il se donne" would simply be translated as "it is given." And even here, where the concept of self is primordial, if I had systematically translated the reflexive *se* by "itself," the text as a whole would have been falsified, undermined, corroded, pockmarked with indigestible *itselves*.

The fact is that the French word *moi* means "me," and *le Moi* is the Ego. Something is lost in translation, but it is a minor mishap compared to the loss of conscience in "consciousness" (*conscience*), and the loss of inordinate nongeographic dimension when *en-deçà*, really a sort of above and beyond, becomes "beneath." And how could I convey the ever-unfolding meaning of *autrui*? And the difference between *les autres* and *autrui*, which operates strongly on the level of everyday discourse and carries smoothly into philosophical thought without losing its biblical reference: "Do unto others . . ."

What is the correct translation of the key Levinassian concept of *visage*? What word could convey the paradox of this face, neither presented nor represented and yet unique and individual, that bears above and beyond, that is, beneath all features the expression of the human condition, that opens being to the ethical dimension beyond being, this visage that is not a face? *Visage* is an ordinary, everyday word. We tell a child to "*se laver le visage*," to wash his face. Levinas gave new, precise meaning to the simple word for face. No doubt the Hebrew word *panim* (always plural) is a source of this concept. Though I wish I could have carried the multiple resonance of *visage* (in French) by using *visage* (in English) I would like to thank Richard A. Cohen for convincing me to follow accepted usage.

These implacable realities, these difficult choices, are presented (*se présentent* = present themselves) to the translator with full force in the early stages, when a text hovers between two languages. Gradually, as they are resolved (as Levinas would say, "with the necessary abuse of language"), the memory of such difficulties fades and almost, but never entirely, disappears. Any or all of them may later be thrown in the translator's face by specialists who would have chosen other solutions. There are indeed a multitude of possible interpretations/translations, none of which can be thoroughly satisfying.

How then are we to honor a great text, a brilliant mind? I think that the challenge lies in finding one's personal point of leverage. And so, within the limits of my intelligence, learning, and experience, I have tried to follow Levinas to the utmost limits of his thought and create an understanding (*entente*) such that every word of the English version is informed by his spirit, and no word is simply stuck on the page as an anonymous mass-produced word. *Se donner, le Moi, la conscience, le visage, en-deça, autrui* . . . these are only words. They must not be stumbling blocks to the re-creation of a work that speaks beyond being. Behind these words, written in French because, by the force of circumstance, "the accidents of history," Levinas left his native Lithuania and settled in France, behind these words are others in German, Greek, and Hebrew; behind these circumstances are others that brought the line of Levinas from Israel to Lithuania by way of, who knows, Spain, Holland . . . ? What I bring to Levinas, in the hopes of compensating for inevitable weaknesses, gaps in knowledge, is my entire life experience, the depth of my own reflections, the possibilities of articulating this experience. For it is so true that it might seem like a commonplace to say that one cannot go any deeper than one's own depth. This or that concept, this or that sentence taken out of context, can be widely debated, and rightfully so. But the intricate dance, the exquisite pathways, the meticulous stitching that shapes and builds and weaves and displays the thought of Levinas is a presence, and I have reached into the depths of his language to bring that presence to life.

Humanism of the Other

✤ ✤ ✤ To Father Herman Leo Van Breda o.f.m.
Founding-director of the Husserl Archives
of Louvain
in remembrance of the Master
in admiration of a work devoted to the Master
tribute of affectionate fidelity
and respectful friendship

Foreword

The foreword, always written after the book, is not always a repetition in approximate terms of the rigorous statement that justifies the book. It may express the first, and urgent, commentary, the first "that is to say"—which is also the first retraction [*dédit*]—of statements where—actual and assembled—the unassemblable proximity of the one-for-the-other, signifying as *Saying* [*Dire*], is absorbed and exposed in the *Said* [*Dit*].

The three essays in this small volume seek that signification. They mark the stages of an "out of date consideration" that is not yet or no longer frightened by the word *humanism*.

Of course, out of date can mean expired, and nothing is preserved from expiration [*péremption*], not even the peremptory. But the out of date where these studies are placed, or toward which they tend, should not be confused with inattention to the dominant opinions of our time, which are so brilliantly and skillfully defended. Here the out of date signifies the *other* of the up to date rather than ignorance and negation of it; the other of what, in the high Western tradition, is commonly called *being-in-act* (however true or untrue this expression may be to the spirit of the Aristotelian notion it claims to transmit); the other of the *being-in-act,* but also its cohort of virtualities that are potentials; the other of being, of the *esse* of being, of the gesture of being, the other of *fully being*—full to overflowing!—stated in this expression *in act;* the other of being in itself—the *inopportune* that interrupts the synthesis of presents that constitutes memorable time.

Being-in-act with nothing that turns up yet or already founders—without dark corners—identity of the identical and the nonidentical—presence without *becoming* or conversion of *becoming* into *presence*—synchrony where the order of the assembled terms does not matter—is this *actuality* of the concept not the famous activity attributed to consciousness? The actuality of total presence excludes or absorbs all alteration; logical exclusion becomes, concretely, representation: retrieval of the present from the past by reminiscence and anticipation of the future [*à venir*] by imagination. Collecting that culminates in consciousness of self or subjectivity. "The original unity of apperception" simply expresses the superlative of being-in-act. Hegel admired the essence of the conception in the *I think* of Kant's transcendental apperception.[1] The application of the *I think* to the diverse of the given, designated in the second edition of the *Critique* as *synthesis speciosa of the imagination*, does not yet take place in the soul, because this application just allows the psychic and the psychological to appear.[2] It is not because the unity of transcendental apperception—or understanding—is spontaneous in the psychological sense that it is action (*Handlung*).[3] It is because it is the actuality of presence that it can make itself spontaneity of the imagination, act on the temporal form of the given, call itself act. The *I* is posited by the *timeless* exercise of that actuality, the necessarily free *I* of classical humanism. Heritage of transcendental philosophy, for Fichte it remains an activity supremely constituting the non-Ego.

Husserl's transcendental reduction tears the pure-Ego away from the psychological, separates it from nature, but lets it live. Intentionality, where the Ego lives, does maintain the structure of act. In Husserlian phenomenology, however, the subjective—transcendental and extramundane—is shown for the first time as irreducible passivity in the notion of passive synthesis. The impressional and the sensible—drawn from an empiricist tradition—are placed in the heart of the Absolute. The concern for synthesis, be it passive, still reflects the exigencies of unity of apperception and actuality of presence; subtle analyses of the ante-predicative still imitate, under the denomination of passives, the models of syntheses of the predicative proposition. But transcendental subjectivity is no longer a simple logical articulation of scientific methods, despite contemporary neo-Kantianism and its influence in Germany. Transcendental subjectivity, living unicity, has its own secret;

intentional acts have their horizons which, though forgotten and not actual, nonetheless codetermine the sense of being; but they deliver their significations only on reflection *turned* toward noesis. No gaze directed at the objective correlate of acts, where, however, these significations signify in the "full noema," could find them, just as it cannot distinguish, in the "total presence" of the objective theme, the "full noema" itself.

However, if the free subject—where the man of humanism placed his dignity—is nothing but a modality of a "logical unity" of "transcendental apperception"—a privileged mode of actuality that must be an end in itself—should we be surprised that, following on Husserl's scrupulous formulation of reduction, the Ego disappears behind—or within—the being-in-act that it was supposed to constitute? More than ever, ultimate intelligibility is the actuality of being-in-act, the coexistence of terms in a theme, the relation, the coherence of one and the other despite their difference, the accord of the different in the present. The system. One signifies the other and is signified by it; each is sign of the other, renouncing what Jean-François Lyotard calls its figure to pass away to the other. The "thinking subject" who seeks this intelligible arrangement interprets itself thenceforth, despite its industrious research and inventive brilliance, as a detour taken by the system of being for its own needs, a detour traced by its terms or structures in order to hitch itself, assemble itself in a great present and, what's more, burst out with truth at all its points, to show off. The subject lets being be.

Of course the subject, by the role incumbent on it, belongs to the gesture of being and by this right manifests itself in turn: to itself and to the social sciences. But it has no significant life beside the truth it serves and where it shows itself. The rest of what is human remains foreign to it.

Intelligibility and relation have a different meaning in the studies collected here. They are still alive with the memory of patricide that cornered Plato. Without that violence, relation and difference were just contradiction and adversity. But they were such in a world of *total presence,* or simultaneity. Doesn't intelligibility go back beneath presence, to the proximity of the other? There, the otherness that infinitely obliges splits time with an unbridgeable *meantime:* "the one" *is* for the other of a being who lets go of itself [*se dé-prend*] without turning into a contemporary of "the other," without taking place next to him in a synthesis exposing itself as a theme; the one-for-the-other as the-one-his-brother's-keeper, as the-one-responsible-for-the-other. Between the one that I am and the other for whom I answer gapes a bottomless difference, which is also the non-indifference of responsibility, significance of signification, irreducible to any system whatsoever. Non-in-difference, which is the very proximity of one's fellow, by which is profiled a base of community between one and the other, unity of the human genre, owing to the fraternity of men.

This proximity does not mean a new "experience" opposed to the experience of objective presence, an experience of the "thou" produced after, or even before, the being's experience of an "ethical experience" in addition to perception. *No, it means casting doubt on* EXPERIENCE *as source of sense,* it means the limit of transcendental apperception, the end of synchrony and its reversible terms; it means the non-priority of the Same and, through all these limitations, it means the end of *actuality,* as if the *inopportune* came to disturb the concordances of representation. As if a strange weakness caused *presence* or being-in-act to shiver and topple. Passivity more passive than the conjoint passivity of the act, which still aspires to the actualization of all its potentials. Synthesis inverted into patience and discourse turned into a voice of "subtle silence" making a sign to Others—to the fellow man, that is, the unencompassable. Weakness without cowardice, like the incalescence of pity. Discharge of a being who lets go of himself [*se dé-prend*]. Perhaps that is what tears are.[4] The swoon of being fainting into humanity, not deemed worthy of the attention of philosophers. But the violence that would not be this repressed sigh or would have strangled it forever does not even belong to the race of Cain; it is the daughter of Hitler, or his adopted daughter.

The contestation of the priority of the Act and its privilege of intelligibility and significance, the rupture in the unity of "transcendental apperception," signifies an order—or disorder—beyond being, before the place before culture. We recognize ethics. We can distinguish in this contact anterior to knowledge, this obsession by the other man, the motivation of many of our everyday tasks and great scientific and political works, but my humanity is not embarked in the history of this culture that *appears,* offering itself to my assumption and making possible the very liberty of that assumption. The other man commands by his face, which is not confined in the form of its appearance; naked, stripped of its form, denuded of its very presence, which would again mask it like its own portrait; wrinkled skin, trace of itself, presence that at every moment is a retreat into the hollow of death with an eventuality of no return. The otherness of the fellow man is this hollow of no-place where, face, he already takes leave [*s'absente*], without promise of return and resurrection.

Waiting for the return in the distress of a possible no return, waiting that is impossible to while away, patience requiring immortality. This is how we say "thou": speaking to the second person, asking or concerned about his health. Requiring immortality despite the certainty that all men are mortal. Demand for immortality. Demand that would already lie in my privileged relation with myself, which excludes me from any genre, showing that humanity is not a genre like animality. An exclusion from the human genre repeated in the death of others, each new death a new "first scandal." These profound observations in Vladimir Jankélévitch's very moving book on death also go back—beyond the undeniable motifs of human exception: dignity of the person, *conatus,* and concern for being in a being conscious of its death—to the impossibility of canceling responsibility for the other, impossibility more impossible than jumping out of one's skin, the imprescriptible duty surpassing the *forces of being.* A duty that did not ask for consent, that came into me traumatically, from beneath all rememberable present, anarchically, without beginning. That came without being offered as a choice, came as election where my contingent humanity becomes identity and unicity, through the impossibility of escaping from election. Duty imposed beyond the limits of being and its annihilation, beyond death, putting being and its resources in deficit. Nameless identity. It says *I* which is identified with nothing that presents itself, if not the very sound of its voice. The "I speak" is understood in all "I do" and even in the "I think" and the "I am." Unjustifiable identity, pure sign made to others, sign made of the very donation of the sign, the messenger being message, the signified sign without figure, without presence, outside the acquired, outside of civilization. Identity immediately posed in the accusative of the "here I am," like a sound audible only in its echo, delivered to the ear without taking satisfaction in the energy of its repercussion.

Paris, 12 March 1972.

❦ ❦ ❦ Signification and Sense

1. Signification and Receptivity

There would seem to be a distinction between the reality given to receptivity and the signification it can acquire. As if experience first offered contents—forms, solidity, roughness, color, sound, flavor, odor, warmth, weight, etc.—and afterward these contents were animated by meta-phors, received a surcharge that carried them *beyond* the given.

This *meta*phor can be attributed either to a defect of perception or its excellence, depending on whether the *beyond* of the metaphor leads to other contents simply absent from the limited field of perception or transcendent with regard to the order of the contents or the given.

This solid rectangular opacity becomes a book only in carrying my thought toward other givens, still or already absent: the author who writes, the readers who read, the bookshelves that hold, etc. All these terms are announced without being given in the solid rectangular opacity imposed on my sight and hands. These absent contents confer signification on the given. But this recourse to absence attests to a failure of perception in its mission of perception, which is to render present, to represent. Because of its finitude, perception missed out on its vocation; so it made up for this *lack* by signifying that which it cannot represent. The act of signifying would be more indigent than the act of perceiving. Rightfully, reality would have immediate signification. Reality and intelligibility would coincide. The identity of things would carry the identity of their signification. For God, who is capable of unlimited perception, there would be no signification distinct from the perceived reality; understanding would be equivalent to perceiving.

Intellectualism—whether rationalist or empiricist, idealist or real-ist—is attached to this conception. For Plato, for Hume, and even for contemporary logical positivists, signification is reduced to the contents given to consciousness. Intuition, in the rectitude of a consciousness receiving givens, remains the source of all signification, whether the givens are ideas, relations, or sensible properties. Significations carried by language must be justified in a reflection on the consciousness that sights them. Any metaphor that language makes possible must come down to the givens that the language is suspected of having wrongfully surpassed. The figurative sense must be justified by the literal sense offered to the intuition.

In *Jardin d'Épicure* Anatole France reduces the saying "The spirit blows where it will" to its elementary signification. He "deflates" the puffed up metaphors that, unwittingly, would have free play in this saying. He goes from the false prestige of language to the atoms of experience. As it happens, they are the atoms of Democritus and Epicurus. Anatole France tries to return from the glare produced by their agglomeration and get back to the dreary rain of atoms that go through spaces and strike the senses.

The simplistic aspect of this empiricism can easily be overcome without losing the essence of the intuitivist or intellectualist conception of signification. Husserl, who incidentally marks the end of this notion of signification, pursues—and this is one of the (perhaps fertile) ambiguities of his philosophy—its intellectualism: *he accounts for significations by a return to the given.* Categorical intuition—the notion by which he breaks with sensualist empiricism—in fact extends the intuitivism of signification. Relations and essences are, in turn, givens. Intuition remains the source of all intelligibility. Sense is given in the very rectitude that characterizes the relation between noesis and noema. Isn't Husserl's transcendental philosophy a kind of positivism that refers, for all signification, to its transcendental inventory? There the hyletic givens and "loans of sense" are meticulously inventoried as if one were handling an investment portfolio. Even that which remains unrealized is somehow given, *en creux,* in an open "signitive" intention, and attested in the noema and the noesis as "unpaid bills." All absence has the given as terminus a quo and terminus ad quem. The expression of significations simply serves to fix or communicate significations justified in intuition. Expression has no function in the constitution or comprehension of these significations.

But the metaphor—the reference to absence—can be considered an excellence pertaining to a different order of pure receptivity. The absence to which the meta-phor leads is not another given, one that is still future or already past. Signification does not console a disappointed perception, *it just makes perception possible.* Pure receptivity, like pure sensibility without signification, would be a myth or abstraction. Sonic contents, such as vowels "bereft of sense," have a "latent birth" in significations; this is already the philosophic lesson of the famous Rimbaud sonnet. No given would bear identity forthwith; none could enter into thought by the effect of a simple shock against the wall of a receptivity. To be given to consciousness, to glimmer for it, the given would have to be previously placed on an illuminated horizon, similar to the word that receives the gift of being understood from a context to which it refers. Signification would be the very illumination of this horizon. But the horizon does not result from an addition of absent givens, because each given already needs a horizon to define and give itself. This notion of horizon, or *world,* conceived on the model of a context and, finally, on the model of a language and culture—with all the historical adventure and "already done" this entails—is then the place where signification is situated.

Words would already be without isolatable significations of the kind found in dictionaries that could be reduced to some sort of contents and givens. They would not be frozen into a literal meaning. In fact there would be no literal meaning. Words would not refer back to contents that they designate but laterally, in the first place, to other words. Despite the mistrust Plato shows for written language (and, in the seventh letter, for all language), he teaches in the *Cratylus* that even the names given to gods—proper nouns conventionally attached as signs to individual beings—refer back through their etymology to other words that are not proper nouns. Moreover, language refers to the positions of the listener and the speaker, that is, to the contingency of their story. To seize by inventory all the contexts of language and all possible positions of interlocutors is a senseless task. Every verbal signification lies at the confluence of countless semantic rivers.

Experience, like language, no longer seems to be made of isolated elements lodged somehow in a Euclidean space where they could expose themselves, each for itself, directly visible, signifying from themselves. They signify from the "world" and from the position of the one who is looking. We will come back to the essential function incumbent on this supposed contingency of position, both in language and experience, if the theory that we are now expounding is to be believed.

It would be an error to conceive as primordial the significations customarily attached to words that serve to express our immediate, sensible experiences. Baudelaire's "correspondences" attest that sensible givens overflow, by their significations, the element where they are supposedly confined. In his excellent work on the notion of the a priori Mikel Dufrenne showed that experiences of springtime and childhood, for example, remain authentic and native beyond human seasons and ages. When another contemporary philosopher speaks of "dusk" or "morning philosophies," the signification of these adjectives does not necessarily refer to our experiences of weather. It is more likely that our experiences of morning and evening delve into the signification that being as a whole bears for us, and the jubilation of mornings and the mystery of dusk are already involved. So we say morning philosophy more authentically than morning freshness! But significations are not limited to any special region of objects, are not the privilege of any contents. They arise precisely in the reference to each other and—let us say here, in anticipation—in the *collection of being* all together around the one who speaks or perceives and who, moreover, is part of the collected being. In a study of Homeric comparisons, Snell (as cited by Karl Löwith) points out that the comparison in the *Iliad* of resistance against attack from an enemy phalanx to the resistance of a rock against assaulting waves is not necessarily an anthropomorphic extension of human behavior to the rock but rather a petromorphic interpretation of human resistance. Resistance is not the prerogative of men or rocks, just as radiance is no more authentically a quality of a morning in May or a woman's face. Signification precedes givens and illuminates them.

Here is where the major justification and the major force of Heidegger's etymologies lie: they lead from the impoverished flat sense of the term that designates, in appearance, a content of exterior or psychological experience, to an overall situation where a totality of experiences are collected to illuminate themselves. The given is presented forthwith *as* this or that; that is, as signification. Experience is a reading, an understanding of sense, an exegesis, a hermeneutic, and not an intuition. *This as that*: signification is not the modification brought to a content existing outside language. Everything remains within a language or within a world, a world whose structure resembles the order of language with possibilities that no dictionary can permanently settle. In the *this as that*, neither the *this* nor the *that* is given forthwith, outside of discourse. In our initial example, this solid rectangular opacity does not subsequently take the sense of *book*; it is already signifying in its supposedly sensible elements. It cuts into the lamplight, the daylight, it reflects the sun that rose or the lamp that was lit and also reflects in my eyes, as the solidity reflects in my hand—not simply to organs that apprehend it *in* a subject and thereby are somehow opposed to the apprehended object but also to beings who are *beside* that opacity, *in the heart of* a world, common both to that opacity, that solidity, those eyes, those hands, and myself as body. At no time would there have been *initial birth of signification from being without signification* and outside a historical position where language is spoken. This is doubtless what was meant when we were taught that language is the habitation of being.

Which, in a movement radically opposite to the one that amused Anatole France, gives us the idea of the priority of a "figurative sense" that does not result from the pure and simple presence of an object placed in front of thought. Objects become significant from language and not language from objects given to thought and designated by words that function as simple signs.

2. Signification, Totality, and Cultural Gesture

The essence of language, to which philosophers henceforth grant a primordial role as marking the very notion of culture, consists in making being in its totality, beyond the *given*, glow. The given takes its signification from that totality.

But the totality that illuminates would not be the total of a sum obtained by a God fixed in his eternity. The totalization of the totality would not resemble a mathematical operation. It would be an unpredictable creative collection or arrangement similar, in its novelty and debt to history, to the Bergsonian intuition. This reference of illuminating totality to the creative gesture of subjectivity marks the originality of the new notion of signification, irreducible to the integration of intuitively given contents, and irreducible to the objectively constituted Hegelian totality. Signification, as illuminating totality necessary to perception itself, is a free creative arrangement: the eye that sees is *essentially* in a body which is also hand and phonetic organ, creative activity by gesture and language. The "position of he who is looking" does not introduce a relative into the supposedly absolute order of the totality projecting onto an absolute retina. The looking *in and of itself* would be relative to a position. Vision *by essence* would be attached to a body and depend on the eye. *By essence* and not only *in fact*. The eye would not be the more-or-less perfected instrument by which, in the human species, the ideal enterprise of vision would empirically succeed in capturing the reflection of being, without shadows or deformities. And these facts—that the totality overflows the sensible given and that vision is embodied—belong to the essence of vision. Its original and ultimate function would not consist in reflecting being as in a mirror. Vision's receptivity should not be interpreted as an aptitude to receive impressions. A philosophy—such as the thought of Merleau-Ponty, which guides the present analysis—was astonished at the marvel of vision attached essentially to an eye. This philosophy thinks the body as inseparable from creative activity, and transcendence as inseparable from bodily motion.

We will now clarify these fundamental notions. The totality of being must produce itself to illuminate the given. It must produce before a being can be reflected in a thought, before a spotlight can illuminate and a curtain rise on the side of being. The function of the one who must be there to "receive the reflection" is at the mercy of that illumination. But that illumination is a process of collection of being. Who operates this collection? It so happens that the subject who is there in front of being to "receive the reflection" is also beside being to operate the collection. This ubiquity is embodiment itself, the marvel of the human body.

Let us admire the reversal of the gnoseologic formula. Here the work of knowledge begins on the side of the object or behind the object, in the backstage of being. Being must first illuminate itself and take signification by referring to this collection, so that the subject can receive it. But it is the embodied subject who, in collecting being, will raise the curtain. The spectator is the actor. Vision is not reduced to receiving the spectacle: it simultaneously operates inside the spectacle it receives.

These operations certainly evoke, in one aspect, the syntheses of understanding that, in transcendental philosophy, make experience possible. And the comparison is all the more justified in that Kant rigorously distinguished syntheses of understanding from intuition, as if, in the realm that concerns us here, he refused to identify the intelligence that one can have of a signification with the vision of any given, be it of superior or sublime rank. But the transcendental operations of understanding do not correspond to the rise of significations in the concrete horizons of perception. Merleau-Ponty called attention to these horizons.

The collection of being that illuminates objects and makes them significant is not some kind of pileup of objects. It corresponds not only to the production of a new type of non-natural beings that are cultural objects—paintings, poems, melodies—but also to the effect of any linguistic or manual gesture of the most ordinary activity, creative in its evocation of former cultural creations. These cultural "objects" collect in totalities the dispersion or heaping of beings. They glow and illuminate, they express or illuminate an era, as in fact we are accustomed to saying. To collect in a totality, that is, to express, that is, to make signification possible—this is the function of the "object-cultural work or gesture." And there a new function of *expression* is established with regard to the functions heretofore attributed to it: either to serve as a means of communication or to transform the world according to our needs. The novelty of this function lies also in the original ontological level on which it is situated. As a means of communication or a mark of our practical projects, expression would flow all in one piece from a thought prior to it; expression would go from the interior toward the exterior. In its new function, taken on the level of cultural "object," expression is no longer guided by prior thought.

The subject ventures by effective word or manual gesture in the density of the pre-existent language and cultural world (that which is familiar to it but is not knowledge/that which is foreign to it but is not ignorance) to which these words and gestures, as embodied, then belong and that they know how to stir and rearrange and reveal only that way, "deep within" the thought that the adventure of the cultural gesture had always already overflowed. Cultural action does not express prior thought; it expresses the being to which, embodied, it already belonged. *Signification can not be inventoried in the interiority of thought.* The thought itself intervenes in the Culture through the verbal gesture of the body that precedes and surpasses it. The objective Culture to which, by verbal creation, it adds something new, illuminates and guides it.

It is obvious then that the language through which signification is produced in being is a language spoken by embodied minds. The embodiment of thought is not an accident that happened to it, that makes its task heavier by deflecting from its rectitude the straight movement by which it sights the object. The body is the fact that thought is immersed in the world that it thinks and consequently expresses this world at the same time as it thinks it. The bodily gesture is not a nervous discharge, it is a celebration of the world, poetry. The body is a sensing sensed; and that is what Merleau-Ponty finds so marvelous about it. Sensed, it nevertheless remains on this side, the side of the subject; but sensing, it is already on that side, the side of objects; thought is no longer paralytic, it is motion, no longer blind, it is creative of cultural objects. It combines the subjectivity of perception (intentionality sighting the object) and the objectivity of expression (operation in the perceived world that creates cultural beings—language, poem, painting, symphony, dance—illuminating horizons). Cultural creation is not added to receptivity, it is the other face. We are not subjects of the world and part of the world from two different points of view; in expression we are at the same time subject and part. To perceive is, by a sort of prolepsis, to receive and express at the same time. By gesture we are able to imitate the visible and *kinesthetically* coincide with the gesture *seen;* in perception *our* body is also the "delegate" of *Being.*

It is obvious that in this whole conception expression defines culture, culture is art, and art or the celebration of being is the original essence of embodiment. Language as expression is above all the creative language of poetry. So art is not the lovely madness of man who takes it in his head to make beauty. Culture and artistic creation are part of the ontological order itself. They are ontological par excellence; they make it possible to comprehend being. So it is no accident that the exaltation of culture and cultures, the exaltation of the artistic aspect of culture, guides contemporary spiritual life and that, beyond the specialized labor of scientific research, museums and theaters like temples in the past make possible communion with being, and that poetry passes for prayer. Artistic creation collects being in signification, bringing the original light that scientific knowledge itself borrows. Thus artistic expression would be an essential event produced in being through artists and philosophers. Then it is not surprising that Merleau-Ponty's thought seemed to develop in the direction of Heidegger. The exceptional position, between the objective and the subjective, occupied by cultural signification, cultural activity that reveals being; the worker of this revelation, the subject, invested by being as servant and guardian—here we meet the schema of the late Heidegger, which is also the fixed idea of all contemporary thought: getting past the subject-object structure. It may be that at the source of all these philosophies stands the Hegelian vision of subjectivity understood as an ineluctable moment of becoming by which being comes out of its obscurity, the vision of a subject aroused by the logic of being.

The symbolism of signification riveted to language, and culture assimilated with language, would in no way pass for defective intuition, for the last resort of experience separated from the plenitude of being that, nevertheless, would be reduced to signs. The symbol is not the shortcut of a pre-existent real presence; it gives more than any receptivity in the world could ever receive. The signified overtakes the given not because it overtakes our ways of grasping it—being deprived of intellectual intuition—but because the signified is of another order than the given, be it prey to a divine intuition. *Receiving givens* would not be the original way of relating to being.

3. Anti-Platonism in Contemporary Philosophy of Signification

The totality of being where being shines forth as signification is not an entity fixed for eternity; it requires arrangement and collection, the cultural act of man. Being as a whole—signification—glows in the works of poets and artists. But it glows in varied ways in the works of varied artists from the same culture, and is expressed diversely in diverse cultures. This diversity of expression does not, in the eyes of Merleau-Ponty, betray being but makes it scintillate with the inexhaustible wealth of its event. Every cultural work goes all the way through being, and leaves it intact. For Heidegger, being is revealed out of the abstruseness and mystery of the unsaid that poets and philosophers bring to word without ever saying all. All the expressions that being received and receives in history would be true, because truth is inseparable from its historical expression and, without its expression, thought thinks nothing. Contemporary philosophy of signification—whether Hegelian, Bergsonian or phenomenological in origin—is thus opposed to Plato on a fundamental point: the intelligible is inconceivable outside the becoming that suggests it. There does not exist any *signification in itself* that a thought could reach by hopping over the reflections—distorting or faithful, but sensible—that lead to it. To reach the intelligible we must cross through history, or relive duration, or go from concrete perception and the language installed in it. All things picturesque in history, all the different cultures, are no longer obstacles that separate us from the essential and the Intelligible; they are the paths by which we can reach it. Furthermore, they are unique pathways, the only possible paths, irreplaceable, and consequently implicated in the intelligible itself!

In the light of contemporary philosophy, and by contrast, we understand more clearly what Plato meant by separation from the intelligible world, beyond the mythical sense attributed to the realism of the Ideas: for Plato, the world of significations precedes the language and culture that express it; it is indifferent to the system of signs that can be invented to make this world present to thought. Consequently, it dominates historical cultures. For Plato there would exist a privileged culture that does approach it and can understand the transitory and

seemingly childish nature of historical cultures; there would exist a culture that consists of depreciating purely historical cultures and in a certain way colonizing the world, beginning with the country where this
revolutionary culture, this philosophy surpassing cultures, arises; there
would exist a culture that would consist of remaking the world according to the timeless order of the Ideas, like the Platonic Republic,
that sweeps away the allusions and alluviums of history, like the Republic that chases the poets of the μίμησις. In fact, the language of
those poets does not function to lead to eternal significations that pre-
exist their expression. Their language is not pure recital of these ideas
ἁπλῆ διήγησις ἀνευ μιμήσεως (*Republic* 394b). It tries to imitate the
direct discourse of countless cultures and countless manifestations in
which each one flourishes. So these poets let themselves be carried
away into the becoming of particularities, strangeness and oddities, inseparable—for the poets of the μίμησις (as for many moderns)—from
the thoughts expressed, which cannot be recited simply. If humanity
were to lose or forget or abolish these particularities, these idioms, it
would lose the invaluable treasures of significations, irrecoverable
without the recovery of all cultural forms, that is, without their imitation.

For contemporary philosophy, signification is not only correlative to
thought and thought is not only correlative to a language that would
make of signification an ἁπλῆ διήγησις. Superimposed on this intellectualist structure of *correlation* between intelligence and the intelligible, which maintains the separation of levels, is a *neighboring* and a
side by side, an *alliance* that unites intelligence and the intelligible on the
unique level of the world, forming the "fundamental historicity" referred to by Merleau-Ponty. So Plato's love of truth, which placed pure
thought in face of signification, turns out to be incestuous disturbance,
because of the consanguinity of intelligence and the intelligible tangled
up in the network of language, arising in expression from which
thought is inseparable. The anti-Platonism of contemporary philosophy lies in the subordination of intellect to expression; the soul-idea
face to face is thereby interpreted as the limit-abstraction of contact
within a common world; the intellect sighting the intelligible would
itself stand on the being that the sighted only claims to illuminate. No

philosophical movement has surpassed contemporary phenomenology in bringing out the transcendental function of the concrete density of our corporal, technological, social and political existence and, thereby, the interference in "fundamental historicity"—in this new *mixed* form—of the transcendental relation and the physical, technological, cultural relations that constitute the world.

We already referred above to the relation between Bergson and phenomenology. Bergson's anti-Platonisim does not lie simply in his general reevaluation of becoming; it is found in the Bergsonian conception of comprehension, which is quite similar to phenomenological anti-Platonism. When Bergson refuses to separate the whole past of a being from the choice that free being would have to make, when he refuses to accept that the problem demanding a decision can be formulated in abstract intellectual terms on which any and all reasonable beings could make a decision, he situates the intelligible in the prolongation of the entire concrete existence of the individual. The signification of the decision to be made cannot be intelligible to anyone but the person who had lived the past leading up to that decision. Signification cannot be directly understood in a flash of light that illuminates and chases the night from which it arises, that it unravels. It needs all the density of the story.

For phenomenologists, as for Bergsonians, signification is not separate from the access leading to it. *Access is part of signification itself.* The scaffoldings are never dismantled. The ladder is never drawn up. Whereas the Platonic soul, liberated from the concrete conditions of its bodily and historical existence, can reach Empyrean heights and contemplate the Ideas, whereas the slave, as long as he "understands Greek" well enough to have a relation with his master, arrives at the same truths as the master, contemporary thinkers ask God himself, if he wants to be a physicist, to go through laboratories, weights and measures, sensible perception and the infinite series of aspects in which the perceived object is revealed.

The most recent, most daring and influential anthropology keeps multiple cultures on the same level. Thus, efforts at political decolonization are connected to an ontology, an idea of being interpreted from multiple multivocal cultural signification. And this multivocity of the sense of being, this essential disorientation, may well be the modern expression of atheism.

4. "Economic" Signification

In fact, the multiplicity of significations that come to reality from culture and cultures is countered by the fixed favored signification that the world acquires according to man's needs. Need raises things simply given to the rank of values. Needs, admirably direct and impatient in their aims, give themselves multiple possibilities of signification solely to be able to choose the unique path to satisfaction. Man confers a unique sense to being by working it, not by celebrating it. In scientific technical culture the ambiguity of being, like the ambiguity of signification, is surmounted. Then, instead of enjoying the play of cultural significations one must, in a concern for truth, release the word from metaphor by creating scientific or algorithmic terminology and insert the real that sparkles with a thousand lights for perception into the perspective of human needs and the action that the Real exerts or endures. It means bringing perception down to science that is justified by the possible transformation of the world, bringing man down to the complexes of psychoanalysis, bringing society down to its economic structures. Sense has to be retrieved everywhere: under signification, under metaphor, under sublimation, under literature. So there would be "serious" real significations, stated in scientific terms, oriented by needs and, in a general way, by economy. Economy alone is truly oriented and signifying. It alone has the secret of a proper sense prior to a figurative sense. Cultural signification detached from this economic sense—scientific and technical—has only symptomatic value, the price of an ornament that suits the needs of the game, wrongful misleading signification exterior to the truth. There can be no doubt about the deeply rationalist aspiration of this materialism, its fidelity to the unity of sense that the multiplicity of cultural significations itself would suppose.

Nevertheless, Bergson and phenomenology have the great merit of showing the metaphoric character of this identification of reality with *Wirklichkeit*. The technical designation of the universe is itself a modality of culture: reduction of the Real to the "Object in general," interpretation of being as if it were meant for the Laboratory and Factory. A scientific technical vision that imposes on needs, modifying, leveling out, and creating them instead of responding to their original rectitude and univocality. Because in reality no human need exists in the univocal state of an animal need. All human needs are culturally interpreted. Only needs approached on the level of underdeveloped humanity can give this false impression of univocality. Besides, it is not certain that the scientific and technological signification of the world can "dissolve" the multiplicity of cultural significations. In fact this seems most doubtful when we observe the dangers weighing on the unity of the new international society placed under the sign of modern scientific and industrial development, and grouping humanity around univocal imperatives of materialism and national particularisms, as if these particularisms themselves answered needs. And of course this robs them of their nature as simple superstructures. The forms in which this search for a unique sense of being based on needs is manifest are acts in view of realization of a society. They are borne by a spirit of sacrifice and altruism that no longer proceeds from these needs (unless we would play on the word "needs [*besoins*]"). The needs that supposedly orient being draw their meaning from an intention that no longer proceeds from these needs. This was already the great lesson of Plato's *Republic:* the State that is based on men's needs cannot subsist nor even arise without philosophers who have mastered their own needs and contemplate the Ideas and the Good.

5. Unique Sense/One-Way

The impossibility of basing the univocal signification of being on materialism—though the attempt is the great honor of materialism—does not, however, compromise the ideal of unity that is the force of the Truth and the hope of understanding among people. The cultural, aesthetic notion of signification could not draw it from itself, nor do without it.

Yes, we are told that cultural significations do not betray being by their pluralism, they simply raise themselves thereby to the measure and *essence* of being, its *way* of being. The way of being *is not* to be rigidified in the Parmenidean sphere, identical to itself, nor to be accomplished and fixed in creature. The totality of being coming from cultures would not in any way be panoramic. There would not be totality but totalities in being. Nothing would encompass them. They would not be subject to any judgment claiming to be final. It is said: being *is* historically, it requires men and their cultural becoming to collect itself. It is said: the unity of being, at any moment, would consist simply in the fact that men, in the penetrability of cultures, understand one another; this penetrability could not be made by the intervention of a common language that, independent of cultures, would translate the proper, ideal articulations of significations, making these individual languages useless after all. In this conception, penetration would be, as Merleau-Ponty says, lateral. In fact it is possible for a Frenchman to learn Chinese and pass from one culture to another without an intermediary Esperanto that would falsify both languages it mediated. However, this eventuality leaves out the need for an *orientation* that in fact leads a Frenchman to learn Chinese instead of claiming it is barbaric (that is, lacking in the true virtues of language), that leads him to prefer words to war. One reasons as if the equivalence of cultures and the discovery of their multiplicity and recognition of their riches were not themselves the effects of an orientation and an unambiguous sense in which humanity stands. One reasons as if the multiplicity of cultures had always been rooted in the era of decolonization, as if misunderstanding, war, and conquest did not flow just as naturally from the proximity of multiple expressions of being, the numerous assemblages or arrangements it takes in various civilizations. One reasons as if peaceful coexistence did not suppose that an orientation is traced in being, endowing it with a unique sense. Must we not, therefore, distinguish significations in their cultural pluralism from the sense, orientation, and unity of being, the primordial event where all the other procedures of thought and all the historical life of being are placed? Do cultural significations arise like commonplace entities within the dispersion of the given? Do they not take signification in a dialogue with that which signifies *of itself:* with others? These original significations would command the collections of being: it would not be the—commonplace—assemblages that, outside all dialogue, would already constitute significations. Do the significations not require a unique sense from which they borrow their significance?

   The world—as soon as one steps away from humble daily tasks— and language—as soon as one steps away from banal conversation—

have lost the *univocality* that would authorize us to ask of them the criteria of what makes sense. Absurdity does not lie in non-sense but in the isolation of countless significations, the absence of a sense that orients them. What is lacking is the sense of the senses, the Rome to which all roads lead, the symphony where all senses become song, the song of songs. Absurdity lies in multiplicity within pure indifference. Cultural significations posed as ultimate are the explosion of a unity. It is not a question of simply setting the conditions in which the facts of our experience or the signs of our language arouse in us a sentiment of comprehension or seem to proceed from a reasonable intention or translate a structured order. It is a question, beyond these logical and psychological problems, of true signification.

This loss of unity was proclaimed—and consecrated in reverse—by the much touted, now hackneyed, paradox of the death of God. So in the contemporary world the crisis of sense is experienced as a crisis of monotheism. A god intervened in human history as a force, sovereign, of course, invisible to the eye and undemonstrable by reason, consequently supernatural, or transcendent, but his intervention took place in a system of reciprocities and exchanges. A system described on a basis of man preoccupied with himself. The god who transcended the world remained united to the world by the unity of an economy. His effects ended up among the effects of all the other forces and mixed with them, in the *miracle*. God of miracles, even in an era when no one expects miracles anymore; a force in the world, magic despite all his morality, morality turning into magic, acquiring magical virtues; a god one comes to as a beggar. Despite the immanence of his revelation, the statute of his transcendence—his new transcendence with regard to the unbroachable transcendence of the Aristotelian god—the statute of this transcendence of the supernatural was never established. Interventions of the supernatural god could, to a certain extent, be counted on and even influenced, like the effects of other wills and forces that preside over events. The denials history inflicted on this economy no more refuted supernatural providence than the misplacement of stars refuted Ptolemy's astronomy. They confirmed it, even at the cost of some new theological "epicycles."

This religion that a person would want for himself instead of feeling himself necessary to the religion, and this god who entered into economic channels—religion and god that in fact did not exhaust the message of Scripture—lost their influence on men. And so the sense of a world perfectly and very simply ordained to this god was lost. We disagree. We do not think that what makes sense can do without God, nor that the idea of Being, or the Being [*l'être*] of beings [*l'étant*], can substitute for God to lead signification to the unity of sense without which there is no sense.

But sense can not be described from what remains an economic idea of God; it is the analysis of sense that should bring forth the notion of God borne within sense. Sense is impossible based on an Ego that exists, as Heidegger says, in such a way "that its existence is an issue for this existence itself."

6. Sense and the Work

Reflection on cultural signification leads to a pluralism lacking in a unique sense. It seemed at one time that economy and technology would trace it. However, if cultural significations can be interpreted as superstructures of the economy, economy in turn borrows its form from culture. The ambivalence of significations attests a disorientation. Let us first remark that this ambiguity seems to respond to a certain philosophic spirit that takes pleasure in a non-polarized ether. Does not sense, as orientation, indicate a thrust, an outside of self toward the *other than self*, whereas philosophy wants to absorb all Other in the Same, and neutralize otherness? Mistrust of any thoughtless gesture, lucidity of old age that absorbs youthful imprudence, Action recuperated in advance in the wisdom that guides it: this could well be the definition of philosophy.

Even if life precedes philosophy, even if contemporary philosophy, which tries to be anti-intellectualist, insists on the anteriority of existence with regard to essence, of life with regard to intelligence, even if Heidegger substitutes "gratitude" toward being and "obedience" for contemplation, contemporary philosophy takes satisfaction [*se com-*

plaît] in the multiplicity of cultural significations; and in the infinite game of art, being is relieved of the weight of its otherness. Philosophy is produced as a form that manifests the refusal of engagement in the Other, a preference for waiting over action, indifference toward others—the universal allergy of the first childhood of philosophers. Philosophy's itinerary still follows the path of Ulysses whose adventure in the world was but a return to his native island—complacency in the Same, misunderstanding of the Other.

But must we renounce knowledge and significations in order to retrieve sense? Must orientation be blind so that cultural significations will take a unique sense and being will recover a unity of sense? But doesn't blind orientation represent the instinctive rather than the human order, where the person betrays his vocation as person by absorbing himself in the law that situates and orients him? Then is it not possible to conceive an orientation—a sense—in being that would reunite univocality and freedom? This at least is the aim of the analysis undertaken here.

First we must clearly establish the conditions of such an orientation. It must be posited as a motion from the identical toward an Other that is absolutely other. It begins in an identical, a Same, an Ego; it is not a "sense of history" that dominates the Ego, because the irresistible orientation of history makes the very fact of motion senseless, the Other already being inscribed in the Same, the end in the beginning. An orientation that goes *freely* from Same to Other is a Work.

Then the Work must not be thought as the apparent agitation of a stock that afterward remains identical to itself, like an energy that remains equal to itself through all its manifestations. Nor must the Work be thought as similar to the technique that, by well-known negativity, transforms a strange world into a world whose otherness is converted to my idea. Both of these conceptions continue to assert being as identical to itself, and reduce its fundamental event to thought that is—and this is the ineffaceable lesson of idealism—thought of itself, thought of thought. The attitude, initially attitude toward the other, becomes, to employ Eric Weil's terminology, totality or category. Whereas *the Work thought radically is a movement of the Same toward the Other that never returns to the Same.* The Work thought all the way through demands a radical generosity of movement which in the Same goes toward the Other. It demands, consequently, *ingratitude* from the Other. Because gratitude would in fact be the return of the movement to its origin.

Moreover, the Work must differ from a game played in pure expense. It is not an undertaking of pure loss. Its identity bordered with nothingness does not suffice to its seriousness. The Work is not pure acquisition of honors, nor pure nihilism. Because the nihilist agent, like a person given to hunting honors, immediately takes himself for term and aim, beneath the apparent gratuity of his action. The Work is a relation with the Other who is reached without showing that he is touched. It is traced outside the "morose delectation" in failure and consolations by which Nietzsche defines Christianity.

However, a departure with no return, that does not fall into the void either, would also lose its absolute *orientation* if it sought compensation in an immediate triumph, if it impatiently awaited the triumph of its cause. The "unique sense/one way" would be inverted into reciprocity. Looking at the work's start and finish, the Agent would resorb it in calculations of deficits and compensations, in cost accounting. It would be subordinated to thought. As absolute orientation toward the Other— as sense—the work is possible only in the patience that, pushed to the limit, signifies that the Agent renounces contemporaneity with its fulfillment, that he acts without entering the Promised Land.

The Future for which such an action acts must be posed as indifferent to my death. The Work, distinct from both games and computations, is being-for-beyond-my-death. Patience does not mean that the Agent tricks his generosity by giving himself a time of personal immortality. To renounce contemporaneity with the triumph of one's work is to glimpse this triumph in a *time without me,* is setting sights on this world without me, setting sights on a time beyond the horizon of my time: eschatology without hope for self or liberation with regard to my time.

Being *for* a time that would be without me, *for* a time after my time, beyond the famous "being-for-death"—this is not a banal thought that extrapolates my own duration, it is passage to the time of the Other. Should we call *eternity* that which makes such a passage possible? Or at least the possibility of sacrifice that goes to the very limit of this passage, discovers the non-inoffensive nature of that extrapolation: being for death in order to be for what is after me.

The work as absolute orientation of the Same toward the Other is a sort of radical youth of the generous impulse. The concept could be captured in a Greek term—liturgy—that in its first signification means the exercise of an office that is not only totally gratuitous but requires from the executant an investment at a loss. For the moment this must be separated from all significations borrowed by whatever positive religion, even if the idea of God should somehow show its trace at the end of our analysis. Further, this uncompensated work, whose result in the Agent's time is not banked on, this work insured only for patience, work exercised in the complete domination and surpassing of my time, this liturgy is not placed as a cult beside "works" and ethics. It is ethics itself.

The relation that we have apparently constructed here is not simply constructed. The total gratuity of Action—gratuity distinct from play—upholds our era even if individuals may not rise to its height; and this signifies the freedom of its orientation. Our era is not defined by the triumph of technology for technology, as it is not defined by art for art's sake, as it is not defined by nihilism. It is action for the world to come, surpassing one's era, it is the surpassing of self that requires the epiphany of the Other, and this is the depth of the thesis upheld in these pages. Léon Blum wrote, in December 1941, as he finished the book written in prison at Bourassol and Fort Pourtalet: "We work in the present, not for the present. How many times in public meetings did I repeat and comment the words of Nietzsche: May the future and the most distant things be the rule of all the present days." It doesn't matter what philosophy Léon Blum used to justify that strange capacity to work without working for the present. The force of his confidence outweighs the force of his philosophy. 1941! A hole in history, a year when all the visible gods had abandoned us, where god was truly dead or had gone back to his irrevelation. A man in prison continues to believe in an unrevealed future and invites us to work in the present for the most distant things of which the present is an irrefutable denial. There is something base and vulgar in an action conceived only for the immediate, that is, for nothing but our lifetime. And there is great nobility in energy liberated from the embrace of the present. To act for distant things at a time when Hitlerism triumphed, in the deaf hours of that night without hours, to act independently of any evaluation of the "forces in presence," was undoubtedly the height of nobility.

7. Sense and Ethics

Sense as the liturgical orientation of the work does not proceed from need. Need opens onto a world that is *for me;* it returns to self. Even when it is sublime, like the need for salvation, it is still nostalgia, homesickness. Need is precisely return, the Ego's anxiety for self, egoism, the original form of identification, assimilation of the world in view of coincidence with self, in view of happiness.

In *Cantique des Colonnes,* Valéry speaks of "desire without deficiency." This is surely a reference to Plato's analysis of pure pleasures, where he finds aspiration conditioned by no prior need. We will take up this term of desire. To a subject turned in on itself and characterized, according to the Stoicist expression, by ὁρμή or the tendency to persist in its being or, according to Heidegger's formulation "one whose existence is an issue for that existence itself," to a subject who so defines himself by concern for self and who, in happiness, fulfills his *for-himself,* we oppose the Desire of the Other that proceeds from a being already satisfied and in that sense independent, and who does not desire for himself. Need of someone who has no more needs, recognized in the need of an Other who is Others, who is not (as in Hobbes and Hegel) my enemy, and not my "complement" as he remains in Plato's *Republic,* constituted because something is lacking in the subsistence of each individual. The Desire for Others—sociality—arises in a being who lacks nothing or, more exactly, arises beyond all that could be lacking or satisfying to him. In Desire the Ego goes out to Others in a way that compromises the sovereign identification of the Ego with oneself whose need is just nostalgia, and that the consciousness of need anticipates. Instead of completing or contenting me the movement toward Others involves me in a contingency that in one aspect didn't concern me and should leave me indifferent: what am I doing in this mess? Where does the shock come from, when I pass by, indifferent, under the gaze of Others? The relation with

Others challenges me, empties me of myself and keeps on emptying me by showing me ever new resources. I did not know I was so rich, but I don't have the right to keep anything anymore. Is the Desire for Others appetite or generosity? The Desirable does not satisfy my Desire, it hollows me, nourishing me somehow with new hungers. Desire turns out to be bounty. There is a scene in *Crime and Punishment* where Dostoyevsky describes Sonia Marmeladova looking with "insatiable compassion" at Raskolnikov in his despair. He does not say "inexhaustible compassion." As if the compassion that goes from Sonia to Raskolnikov were a hunger that Raskolnikov's presence nourished beyond all saturation, by increasing that hunger, infinitely.

The Desire for Others that we feel in the most common social experience is fundamental movement, pure transport, absolute orientation, sense. All analysis of language in contemporary philosophy emphasizes, and rightfully so, its hermeneutic structure and the cultural effort of the embodied being who expresses himself. Hasn't the third dimension been forgotten? The direction toward the Other who is not only collaborator and neighbor of our cultural work of expression or client of our artistic production, but interlocutor: the one to whom expression expresses, for whom celebration celebrates, he who is both term of an orientation and first signification. In other words, before it is celebration of being, expression is a relation with the one to whom I express the expression and whose presence is already required so that my cultural gesture of expression can be produced. The Other who faces me is not included in the totality of being that is expressed. He arises behind all collection of being, as the one to whom I express what I express. I find myself facing the Other. He is neither a cultural signification nor a simple given. He is, primordially, *sense* because he lends it to expression itself, because only through him can a phenomenon such as signification introduce itself, of itself, into being.

The analysis of Desire, which we first carefully distinguished from need, Desire, which traces sense in being, will be clarified by an analysis of the otherness toward which Desire tends.

The manifestation of the Other is of course produced, first of all, in the way all signification is produced. The Other is present in a cultural whole, illuminated by that whole just as a text by its context. The manifestation of the whole ensures its presence. It is illuminated by the light of the world. Comprehension of the Other is therefore a hermeneutic, an exegesis. The Other gives itself in the concrete of the totality to which it is immanent and that—corresponding to the remarkable analyses of Merleau-Ponty on which we have widely drawn in the first sections of this study—our cultural initiative—artistic, linguistic, or corporal gesture—expresses and unveils.

But the epiphany of the Other bears its own significance, independent of the signification received from the world. The Other not only comes to us from a context but signifies by itself, without that mediation. The cultural signification that is in a way revealed, and reveals, *horizontally;* that reveals itself from the historical world to which it belongs; that, as phenomenology expresses it, reveals the horizons of this world; this mundane signification is disturbed and upset by another presence, abstract (or more exactly, absolute), non-integrated in the world. That presence consists in coming to us, *making an entry.* Which can be stated thus: the *phenomenon* that is the apparition of the Other is also *face;* or again (to show this entry at every instant new in the immanence and essential historicity of the phenomenon), the epiphany of the face is *visitation.* Whereas the phenomenon is already, on whatever score, image, captive manifestation of its mute plastic form, the epiphany of the face is alive. Its life consists in undoing the form where every *being* [*étant*], when it enters into immanence—that is, when it exposes itself as theme—is already dissimulated.

The Other who manifests himself in the face pierces, in a way, his own plastic essence, like a being who opens the window where, nevertheless, his face is already traced. His presence consists in divesting himself of the form that nevertheless already manifested him. His manifestation is a surplus on the inevitable paralysis of manifestation. This is what we describe with the words: the face speaks. The manifestation of the face is the first discourse. Speaking is first and foremost this way of coming from behind one's appearance, behind one's form; an opening in the opening.

So the visitation of the face is not the unveiling of a world. In the concreteness of the world, the face is abstract or naked. It is denuded of its own image. By the nudity of the face, nudity in itself is simply possible in the world.

The nudity of the face is a stripping with no cultural ornament—an absolution—a detachment of its form in the heart of production of form. The face *enters* our world from an absolutely foreign sphere, that is, precisely, from an ab-solute, which is in fact the name of the completely foreign. The signification of the face in its abstraction is, in the literal sense of the term, extraordinary, exterior to all order, to all world. How is such a construction possible? How is it that the coming of the Other, the visitation of the face, the absolute, cannot convert—in any way—into revelation, be it symbolism or suggestion? How can the face not be simply *true representation* where the Other renounces his otherness? To answer that we must study, in concluding, the exceptional significance of the trace and the personal "order" where such a signification is possible.

For the moment let us emphasize the sense entailed by the abstraction or nudity of the face that pierces the order of the world, and the upheaval of consciousness that responds to this "abstraction." Stripped of its form, the face is chilled to the bone in its nakedness. It is a desolation. The nakedness of the face is destitution and already supplication in the rectitude that sights me. But this supplication is an obligation. Humility unites with elevation. And announces thereby the ethical dimension of visitation. Whereas true *representation* remains the possibility of appearance, whereas the world that collides with thought can do nothing against *free thinking* able to refuse itself from within, taking refuge in itself, remaining precisely *free thinking* in face of the true, able to go back to itself, reflect on itself and claim to be the origin of that which it receives, able to master by memory that which precedes it, whereas free thinking *stays the Same,* the face imposes on me and I cannot stay deaf to its appeal, or forget it, what I mean is I cannot stop being responsible for its desolation. Consciousness loses its first place.

Thus, the presence of the face signifies an irrefutable order—a commandment—that arrests the availability of consciousness. Consciousness is challenged [*mise en question*] by the face. The challenge does not come from awareness of that challenge. The "absolutely other" is not reflected in consciousness. It resists to such an extent that even its resistance is not converted into contents of consciousness. The visitation is the upset of the very egoism of the Ego that upholds that conversion. The face disorients the intentionality that sights it.

This is a challenge of consciousness, not a consciousness of the challenge. The Ego loses its sovereign coincidence with self, its identification where consciousness comes back triumphantly to itself to reside in itself. In the face of the obligation of the Other, the Ego is banished from that repose, is not the already glorious consciousness of this exile. All complacency destroys the rectitude of the ethical movement.

But the challenge to that naive savage liberty for self, sure of its refuge in itself, is not reduced to a negative movement. The challenge to self is precisely reception of the absolutely other. The epiphany of the absolutely other is face where the Other hails me and signifies to me, by its nakedness, by its destitution, an order. Its presence is this summons to respond. The Ego does not only become conscious of this necessity to respond as if it were a demand or a particular duty it must decide on. The Ego is through and through, in its very position, responsibility or diacony, as in chapter 53 of Isaiah.

To be Me/Ego thenceforth signifies being unable to escape from responsibility, as if the whole edifice of creation stood on my shoulders. But the responsibility that empties the Ego of its imperialism and egoism—be it egoism of salvation—does not transform it into a moment of the universal order; it confirms the uniqueness of the Ego. The uniqueness of the Ego is the fact that no one can answer in my stead.

Discovering such an orientation for the Ego means identifying Ego and morality. The Ego is infinitely responsible in face of the Other. The Other who incites this ethical movement of consciousness, who deregulates the good conscience of the coincidence of Same with self, includes a surplus that is inadequate to intentionality. This is Desire, burning with a fire that is not need extinguished by saturation, thinking beyond what one thinks. Because of this unassimilable surplus, because of this *beyond,* we call the relation that attaches the Ego to Other: the idea of Infinity.

The idea of Infinity is Desire. It consists, paradoxically, in thinking more than is thought while keeping it immeasurable with regard to thought, and entering into relation with the ungraspable while maintaining its status as ungraspable. Infinity is not correlative to the idea of Infinity, as if that idea were an intentionality *accomplishing itself* in its "object." The marvel of infinity in the finitude of thought is an upheaval of intentionality, an upheaval of this appetite for light that is intentionality; contrary to saturation where intentionality is pacified, Infinity disorients its Idea. The Ego, in relation with Infinity, is the impossibility of stopping the forward march, the impossibility, as Plato expressed it in the *Phaedo*, of deserting one's post; it is, literally, no time to look back, no way to escape responsibility, no inner hiding place to go back into self; it is marching straight ahead without concern for self. Increase of obligations with regard to self: the more I face up to my responsibilities the more I am responsible. Power made of "powerlessness"—that is the challenge to consciousness and its entry into a contingency of relations that clash with unveiling.

There, in the relation with the face—the ethical relation—the rectitude of an orientation or sense is traced. The *consciousness* of philosophers is essentially reflective. Or at least consciousness is grasped by philosophers in the moment of its return, which is taken for its birth. In its spontaneous pre-reflective movements it already casts a sidelong glance, they believe, toward its origin, and measures the path covered. That is where its initial essence would reside: critique, mastery of self, analysis and decomposition of all signification that overflows self. Well, responsibility is definitely not blind or amnesiac; through all the movements of thought where it unfurls it is carried by an extreme urgency or, more exactly, coincides with it. What was just described as a "no time to look back" is not the happenstance of an awkward or unfortunate consciousness "overflowed by events," or that "can't manage." It is the absolute rigor of an attitude without reflection, a primordial rectitude, a *sense* in being. "Where does it come from, this resistance of the unreflected to reflection?" Merleau-Ponty asked at Royaumont in April 1957, referring to problems posed by Husserl's theory of phenomenological reduction. Our analysis of *sense* may well answer this fundamental question that Merleau-Ponty refused to settle by simple recourse to the finitude of the subject, incapable of total reflection. "Turn to the truth with all one's soul"—Plato's recommendation is not simply a lesson in common sense, preaching effort and sincerity. Is it not aimed at the ultimate most underhand reticence of a soul that, in the face of the Good, would persist in reflecting on Self, thereby arresting the movement toward Others? Is not the force of that "resistance of the unreflected to reflection" the Will itself, anterior and posterior, alpha and omega to all Representation? Then is the will not thorough humility rather than will to power? Humility not to be confused with an ambiguous negation of Self, already prideful of its virtue which, on reflection, it immediately recognizes in itself. But humility of one who "has no time" to turn back to self, who takes no steps to "deny" the self, if not the abnegation of the Work's rectilinear movement toward the infinity of the Other.

To affirm such an orientation and such a sense, to place a consciousness without reflection above and below all reflections, to surprise in the depth of the Ego an unambiguous sincerity and a servant's humility that no transcendental method could either corrupt or absorb, is to ensure the necessary conditions of the "beyond the given" that shows up in all signification, of the *meta*-phor that animates it, a marvel of language whose "verbal origin" will be endlessly denounced by philosophic analysis, without destroying the evident intention that penetrates it. Whatever its philological, social or psychological history, the *beyond* that the metaphor produces has a sense that transcends that history; the illusionist power with which language is endowed must be recognized; lucidity does not abolish the beyond of those illusions. It is of course the role of reflection to bring significations back to their subjective sources, subconscious or social or verbal, to tally their transcendental inventory. However, this method, legitimate for destroying many prestiges, already precludes an essential result: it prohibits in advance all transcendent sight [*visée*] in signification. Before research begins, the method converts all *Other* into *Same,* though Reflection in its own purifying work will employ these notions—if only the *beyond* with regard to which immanence is situated—which, in the absence of the sincerity and rectitude of "consciousness with no return," have no signification. Nothing that is sublime can do without verbal, social, or psychological sources, except enhancement [*sublimation*] itself.

But this consciousness "without reflection" is not simply pre-reflective naïve spontaneous consciousness; it is not pre-critical. Discovering the orientation and unique sense in the moral relation is precisely placing the Ego as already challenged by the Other it desires and, consequently, as criticized in the rectitude of its movement. That is why the challenge of consciousness is not, initially, consciousness of this challenge. That conditions this. How would spontaneous thought turn back if the Other, the Exterior, did not challenge it? And how, in a concern for total Critique entrusted to reflection, would the new naïveté of reflection rise up, lifting the premier naïveté? Well, the Ego erodes its dogmatic naïveté in the face of the Other who demands more than it can spontaneously give.

But the "term" of such a movement, both critical and spontaneous—and which is not, strictly speaking, a term, because it is not an end but the principle calling for a Work without compensation, a liturgy—is no longer called being. And that is where one might see how a philosophical meditation could find it necessary to resort to notions such as Infinity or God.

8. Before Culture

We will conclude by saying that signification is situated before Culture and Aesthetics; it is situated in Ethics, presupposition of all Culture and all signification. Morality does not belong to Culture; it allows us to judge culture, to evaluate the dimension of its elevation. Elevation ordains being.

Elevation introduces a sense into being. This is already experienced in the human body. It leads human societies to erect altars. It is not because men experience verticality in their bodies that the human is placed under the sign of elevation, it is because being is ordained by elevation that the human body is placed in a space where top and bottom are distinguished and the sky is discovered, the sky that Tolstoy's Prince André described—with not a word about colors—as elevation, pure elevation.

It is extremely important to stress the anteriority of sense with regard to cultural signs. To attach all signification to culture, making no distinction between signification and cultural expression, between signification and art that prolongs cultural expression, is to recognize that all cultural personalities realize the Mind by the same rights. Then no signification could be detached from those countless cultures that would allow us to make judgments on them. Then universality could be only, as Merleau-Ponty expresses it, lateral. This universality means that we can go from one culture and penetrate another, as one goes from one's mother tongue to learn another language. The idea of a universal grammar and an algorithmic language built on the skeleton of that grammar must be abandoned. No direct or privileged contact with the world of Ideas is possible. Such a conception of universality translates the radical opposition, characteristic of our times, against cultural expansion by colonization. Culture and colonization do not go together. We would be at the antipodes of what Léon Brunschvicg (and Plato hostile to the poets of the μίμησις) taught us. The progress of the Western conscience no longer means purifying thought of cultural alluviums and language particularisms that, far from signifying the intelligible, perpetuate childishness. Not that Léon Brunschvicg taught us something other than generosity; but he conceived that generosity and the dignity of the Western world as liberating the truth from its cultural presuppositions and going, with Plato, toward significations themselves, separated from becoming. The danger of such a conception is clear. The emancipation of minds can be a pretext for exploitation and violence. Philosophy had to denounce the ambiguity and show that significations arising on the horizon of cultures, and even the excellence of Western culture, are culturally and historically conditioned. So philosophy had to join up with contemporary anthropology. Behold Platonism defeated! But defeated in the name of the very generosity of Western thought that, perceiving the *abstract* man in men, proclaimed the absolute value of the individual and encompassed in the respect granted to him the cultures where these individuals stood and expressed themselves. Platonism is defeated using the very means it furnished to the universal thought derived from Plato, the decried Western civilization that knew how to understand particular cultures that never understood anything about themselves.

The world created by this saraband of countless equivalent cultures, each one justifying itself in its own context, is certainly dis-Occidentalized; however, it is also disoriented. To apperceive for signification a situation that precedes culture, to apperceive language from revelation of the Other—who is at the same time the birth of morality—in the gaze of man sighting a man precisely as abstract man disengaged from all culture in the nakedness of his face, means returning in a new way to Platonism. It also allows for ethical judgments of civilizations. Signification, the intelligible, is being showing itself in its nonhistorical simplicity, its absolutely irreducible unqualifiable nakedness, existing "before" history and "before" culture. Platonism, as assertion of the human, independent of culture and history, is found in Husserl, in his opinionated way of postulating phenomenological reduction and constitution (by rights at least) of the cultural world in the intuitive transcendental consciousness. One is not obliged to follow the same path Husserl took to reach this Platonism. We think we have found the rectitude of signification by another method: intelligible manifestation is produced in the rectitude of morality and in the Work, marking the limits of historical comprehension of the world and the return of Greek wisdom, though mediated by the entire development of contemporary philosophy.

Neither things nor the perceived world nor the scientific world allow us to connect with the standards of the absolute. Those are all cultural Works, bathed in history. But moral standards are not embarked in history and culture. They are not even islets poking up in it, because they make all signification possible, even cultural signification, and they make it possible to judge Cultures.

9. The Trace

However, the notion of sense developed from the epiphany of face, which allowed us to assert it "before history," presents a problem that, in closing, we would like to attempt to resolve.

This "beyond" from which the face comes and that sets consciousness in its rectitude, is it not in turn an unveiled understood idea?

If the extraordinary experience of Entry and Visitation maintains its significance, it is because the *beyond* is not a simple background from which the face solicits us, not an "other world" behind the world. The *beyond* is precisely beyond the "world," that is, beyond all unveiling;

like the One of the first hypothesis in *Parmenides,* transcending all knowledge, be it symbolic or signified. "Neither similar nor dissimilar, neither identical nor non-identical," says Plato of the One, excluding it precisely from all revelation, even indirect revelation. The symbol would bring the symbolized down to the world where it appears. Then what can be this relation with an absence radically removed from unveiling and dissimulation, and what is this absence that makes visitation possible but is not reduced to obscurity, because this absence includes a significance, a significance by which the Other is not converted into Same?

The face is abstract. This abstraction certainly does not correspond to the raw sensible given of the empiricists. Nor is it an instantaneous cut in time, where time would "cross" eternity. The instant pertains to the world; it is a cut that does not bleed. Whereas the abstraction of the face is visitation and advent that disturbs immanence without being set in the horizons of the World. Its abstraction is not obtained from a logical process going from the substance of beings, from the particular to the general. On the contrary, it goes toward beings but is not engaged with them, retires from them, is ab-solved. Its wonder lies in this *elsewhere* whence it comes and where it already retires. But this coming from *elsewhere* is not a *symbolic reference* to this *elsewhere* as to a term. The face presents itself in its nakedness; it is not a concealing— but thereby indicating—form, a base; it is not a hiding—but thereby betraying—phenomenon, a thing in itself. Otherwise the face would be confounded with a lack that precisely presupposes it. If signifying were equivalent to indicating, the face would be insignificant. And Sartre, though stopping short of a full analysis, makes the striking observation that the Other is a pure hole in the world. The Other proceeds from the *absolutely Absent.* Its relation with the *absolutely Absent* whence it comes does not *indicate,* does not *reveal* that *Absent* and yet the Absent has signification in the face. But this significance is not a way for the *Absent* to give itself *en creux* in the presence of the face, which would bring us back again to a kind of unveiling. The relation that goes from the face to the Absent is outside of all revelation and all dissimulation—a third path excluded by these contradictories. How is this third path possible? But are we not still looking at that from which the face proceeds as sphere, as place, as world? Have we been thoroughly true to the prohibition against seeking the beyond as a world behind our world? In which case the order of being would again be supposed as including no status other than that of revealed or dissimulated. In being, revealed transcendence inverts into immanence; the extraordinary is inserted into an order; the Other is absorbed in the Same. Do we not respond in the presence of the Other to an "order" whose significance remains irreversible derangement, absolutely completed past? Such is the significance of the trace. The beyond whence comes the face signifies as the trace. The face is in the trace of the absolutely completed, absolutely past Absent, retired in what Paul Valéry calls "old olden days, never olden enough," that no introspection could discover in Self. The face is precisely the unique opening where the significance of the trans-cendent does not cancel out transcendence to make it enter into an immanent order; on the contrary it is where trans-cendence refuses immanence precisely as ever *completed* transcendence of the transcendent. The relation between signified and signification is, in the trace, not a correlation but *irrectitude* itself. The purportedly mediate and indirect relation of the sign to the signified is of the order of *correlation* and, consequently, still rectitude and thus unveiling that neutralizes trans-cendence. The significance of the trace puts us in a "lateral" relation, inconvertible into rectitude (which is inconceivable in the order of unveiling and being) and responding to an irreversible past. No memory could follow on the trace of this past. It is an immemorial past, and perhaps that too is eternity whose significance obstinately throws back to the past. Eternity is the very irreversibility of time, source and refuge of the past.

But if the significance of the trace is not immediately transformed into rectitude that still marks the sign that reveals and introduces the Absent signified in immanence, it is because the trace signifies beyond being. The personal "order" to which the face obliges us is beyond being. *Beyond being is a Third person* who is not defined by the Oneself, by ipseity. He is the possibility of the third direction of radical *irrectitude* that escapes the bipolar game of immanence and transcendence proper to being, where immanence always wins out over transcendence. The profile taken by the irreversible past, through the trace, is the profile of the "He."[1] The *beyond* whence comes the face is in the third person. The pronoun "He" expresses its inexpressible irreversibility, that is, already having avoided all revelation as all dissimulation and in this sense absolutely unencompassable or absolute, transcendence in an ab-solute past. The illeity of the third person is—the condition of irreversibility.

The third person who, in the face, has already withdrawn from all revelation and all dissimulation—who has passed—this illeity is not a "less than being" with regard to the world where the face penetrates; it is all the enormity, all the immensity, all the Infinity of the absolutely Other, escaping ontology. The supreme presence of the face is inseparable from that supreme irreversible absence that founds the very eminence of visitation.

If the significance of the trace consists in signifying without making appear, if it establishes a relation with illeity—a relation, personal and ethical, a relation, obligation, that does not unveil—if, consequently, the trace does not belong to phenomenology, to comprehension of *appearance* and *dissimulation,* it could at least be approached by another path, by situating that significance from the phenomenology it interrupts.

The trace is not just a sign like any another. But it does also function as a sign. It can be taken for a sign. A detective investigates everything that stands out on the crime scene as a revelatory sign of the criminal's voluntary or involuntary work, the hunter follows the trace of the game that reflects the activity and the path taken by the animal he is tracking, the historian discovers ancient civilizations on the horizons of our world from vestiges of their existence. Everything lines up in order in a world where each thing reveals the other or is revealed with regard to it. But the trace thus taken as a sign still has something exceptional compared to other signs: it signifies outside of all intention of making a sign and outside of any project that would sight it. When one "pays by check" in a commercial transaction so as to leave a trace of payment, the trace is inscribed in the very order of the world. However, the authentic trace disturbs the world's order. It is "superimposed." Its original significance is designed in the imprint left by the one who wanted to erase his traces in an attempt, for example, to accomplish the perfect crime. The one who left traces while erasing his traces didn't want to say or do anything by the traces he leaves. He irreparably disturbed order. Because he passed absolutely. Being, as *leaving a trace*, is passing, leaving, absolving oneself.

But every sign, in this sense, is trace. In addition to what the sign signifies, it is the past of the one who delivered the sign. The significance of the trace is parallel to the significance of the sign sent as communication. The sign stands in that trace. Significance in a letter, for example, would lie in its writing and style, in everything by which in the sending of the message received from the letter's language and sincerity, someone purely and simply passes by. Again, that trace can be taken for a sign. A graphologist, an expert in style, a psychoanalyst can interpret the singular significance of the trace and query the locked-up unconscious but real intentions of the one who delivered the message. But that which remains specifically trace in the graphics and style of the letter does not signify any of those intentions or qualities, does not reveal or hide anything at all. In the trace an absolutely completed past passed. In the trace is sealed its irreversible completion. The unveiling that restitutes the world and brings back to the world, that is proper to a sign or signification, is abolished in that trace.

But then isn't the trace the weight of being itself, outside of acts and language, heavy not by its presence that ranges it in the world but by its very irreversibility, its ab-solution? The trace would be the very indelibility of being, its all-mightiness with regard to all negativity, its immensity that cannot be confined in self and is somehow too big for discretion, for interiority, for a Self. And in fact we want to say that the trace does not put in relation with what would be less than being; it obliges with regard to Infinity, the absolutely Other. But this superiority of the superlative, this elevation, this constant elevation to power, this exaggeration or this infinite surpassing—and, let us say the word, this divinity—are not deduced from the Being of the being [*l'être de l'étant*], nor from its revelation—be it contemporary with an abstruseness—nor from "concrete duration." They are significant from a past which is neither indicated nor signaled in the trace, but where it still disturbs order, coinciding neither with revelation nor dissimulation. The trace is the insertion of space in time, the point where the world leans toward a past and a time. This time is retreat of the Other and, consequently, in no way degradation of duration, which is intact in memory. The superiority does not lie in a presence in the world but in an irreversible transcendence. It is not a modulation of the Being of the being. As *He* and third person, it is somehow outside the distinction between Being and beings. Only a being transcending the world—an ab-solute being—can leave a trace. The trace is the presence of that which, strictly speaking, has never been there, that which is always past. Plotinus believed that proceeding from the One compromised neither the immutability nor the ab-solute separation of the One. It is that situation, at first purely dialectic and quasi verbal (and which is repeated on the subject of the Intelligence and the Soul remaining close to their principle in their upper part and only inclining by their lower parts—which is again iconography) that the exceptional significance of the trace delineates in the world. "When it concerns a principle anterior to beings, the One, he stays in himself; but even though he stays, it is not something different from him that produces beings corresponding to him, he suffices to engender them. . . . here, the trace of the One brings to birth the essence[,] and being is but the trace of the One" (*Aeneiads,* 5.5).

That which in each trace of an empirical passage, beyond the sign it may become, preserves the specific significance of the trace, is possible only by its situation in the trace of this transcendence. The position in the trace that we call illeity does not begin in things; they in themselves do not leave a trace but produce effects, that is to say, remain in the world. One stone scratched another. The scratch can of course be taken for a trace: in reality, without the man who held the stone, the scratch is nothing but an effect. It is no more a trace than a brush fire is the trace of thunder. Cause and effect, even when separated by time, belong to the same world. <u>All that is in things is exposed, even their unknown; the traces that mark them are part of that plenitude of presence, their history has no past.</u> The trace as trace does not only lead to the past it is the very pass to a past more distant than all past and all future that still range themselves in my time, toward the past of the Other where eternity is designed, absolute past that reunites all times.

The absolute of the presence of the Other that justified the interpretation of his epiphany in the exceptional rectitude of thou-ness [*tutoiement*] is not the simple presence where, in the last analysis, things are also present. Their presence still belongs to the present of *my* life. All that constitutes my life, with its past and future, is collected in the present where things come to me. But the face glows in the trace of the Other: that which is presented there is absolving itself from my life and visits me as already ab-solute. Someone already passed. His trace does not *signify* his past, as it does not *signify* his labor, or his enjoyment in the world, it *is* disturbance itself, imprinting itself (one is tempted to say *engraving*) with irrefutable gravity.

The *illeity of that He,* is not the *that* of a thing at our disposal; Buber and Gabriel Marcel rightfully preferred *Thou* to describe the human encounter. The movement of the encounter is not added to the immobile face. It is in this face itself. The face is, in and of itself, visitation and transcendence. But the face, fully open, can at the same time be in itself, because it is in the trace of illeity. Illeity is the origin of the otherness of being, in which the *in itself* of objectivity participates by betraying it.

The God who passed by is not the model of which the face would be the image. To be in the image of God does not signify being the icon of God, but finding oneself in his trace. The revealed God of our Judeo-Christian spirituality preserves all the infinity of his absence which is in the personal "order." He shows himself only in his trace, as in chapter 33 of Exodus. Going toward him is not following this trace that is not a sign. It is going toward Others who stand in the trace of illeity. It is by that illeity, situated beyond the calculations and reciprocities of the economy of the world, that being has sense. Sense that is not a finality.

Because there is no end, no term. The desire of the absolutely Other is not, like a need, extinguished in pleasure.

✿ ✿ ✿   Humanism and An-Archy

Ich liebe den, dessen Seele uebervoll ist, so dass
er sich selber vergisst, und alle Dinge in ihm sind:
so werden alle Dinge sein Untergang.
—Nietzsche, *Zarathustra*, Prologue 4

1

The crisis of humanism in our times undoubtedly originates in an experience of human inefficacy accentuated by the very abundance of
our means of action and the scope of our ambitions. In a world where
things are in place, where eyes, hands and feet can find them, where
science extends the topography of perception and praxis even if it
transfigures their space; in the places that lodge the cities and fields that
humans *inhabit,* ranking themselves by varied groupings among the
beings; in all this reality "in place," the misconstruction [*contre-sens*]
of vast failed undertakings—where politics and technology result in
the negation of the projects they guide—teaches the inconsistency of
man, mere plaything of his works. The unburied dead of wars and
death camps accredit the idea of a death with no future, making tragi-
comic the care for one's self and illusory the pretensions of the *rational
animal* to a privileged place in the cosmos, capable of dominating and
integrating the totality of being in a consciousness of self.

   And consciousness of self, itself, disintegrates. Psychoanalysis attests
to the instability and fallaciousness of the coincidence of self in the cogito, which however should stop the impostures of the evil genius and
restore good-old-days security to a universe that has become wary on all
sides. The coincidence with self in consciousness where, since Descartes,
being *is,* shows itself to Others (and, after the fact, to the subject itself)
as played or worked by impulses, influences, a language that composes
a mask called a person, someone or no one [*la personne ou personne*],

at the limit a personality endowed with purely empirical consistency. Then the world based on the cogito appears human, too human—to the point of having to look for truth in *being,* in a somehow superlative objectivity, pure of all "ideology," without human traces.

One may of course wonder by what spirit of inconsequence antihumanism can still hold for man the discovery of true knowledge; doesn't knowledge, in the last analysis, pass through consciousness of self? The social sciences—which consider nothing more doubtful than an Ego that listens to itself and questions itself (while its being would be going on outside of it), which consider nothing more horrible than the swarm of cultural significations approached from the interior by a subjectivity (whereas their formal expression simplifies and explains them)[1]—do these social sciences not draw on the mediation of a man of science?

But these old objections, certainly known to sociology and psychoanalysis of knowledge, do not have the last word. Because the formalist "refutation" that claims to triumph over subjectivist relativism (contesting subjectivity means asserting the value of the subjectivity that does the contesting!) does not escape the skeptical contestation reborn from its ashes, as if it were a discourse without a last word, as if the logos, which in itself is beginning, origin, ἀρχή—correlative of the void without a past of freedom—were constantly submerged here by the preoriginal, as if subjectivity were not freedom of adhering to a term presented to it but passivity more passive than passivity of receptivity. The latter is again initiative of reception, able to assume that which collides with it. Consequently, it crosses the present of the logos or restores it to memory.[2] In other words, the refutation of subjectivist relativism in the traditional form does not take into account the crisis it surmounts and believes itself in possession of the logos that, for an instant of ontological syncope, the meantime of nowhere, it had lost. By surmounting the relativism of the human it operates a recuperation. The truth obtained as if by ricochet in the explosion of truths and by the wear and tear of the real "right side out" is like the wrong side of the True. It's as if, in metaphysics, the right side and the wrong side were the same. That is undoubtedly the sense of Husserl's objection to Descartes when he reproaches him for identifying the "I am" of the cogito with the exis-

tence of a soul belonging to the world, that is, situating the absolute, uncovered in the destruction of the world, among the things of the world,
as if they had never been engulfed in the "nowhere," as if their sus-
pension had been contingent, as if the being that came out of a coma
in the cogito were still the same as the one that fell into it. Misunderstanding, as Jeanne Delhomme would say, of the *modality*, of what Heidegger calls the history of being. It makes possible, from the cogito, the
return of God and the world, deduced according to traditional standards, whereas Kant and Husserl seek a new mode of foundation in
the transcendental deduction of the object and in the ἐποχή of phenomenological reduction. This is something like a consciousness that
thenceforth the foundation of being—metaphysics—*turns inside out*,
is not done in being, is thought by ulterior motives [*arrière-pensées*] at
the back of thoughts healthily attached to being. Isn't the theme of the
end of metaphysics, which is concomitant with the theme of the end
of humanism, a way of saying this "reversal"? In fact, in our times, metaphysics keeps on ending and the end of metaphysics is our metaphysics,
unavowed, because unequal to any avowal.

Nevertheless, the inconsequence of denouncing the absolute of the
human in the name of evidence brought forth by the social sciences—
where man is not only object but also subject—can pass for apparent.
It would suffice to show the purely operative, temporary role of man
in the unfolding and manifestation of a group of terms that *make a system*. Beyond the possibly "ideological" "objectivity" an order would
be manifest where subjectivity is none other than the detour taken by
the manifestation or intelligibility or truth of the order, in virtue precisely of that order. It is not man with any proper vocation who invents
or seeks or possesses the truth. It is truth that arouses and holds man
(without holding to him), a path where formal or logico-mathematical
type structures enter to range and place themselves according to their
ideal architecture, rejecting human scaffoldings that permit edification.
Even if man's existence—the being-there—consisted in existing in
view of that existence itself, that *ex-sistence*, all those movements and
reversals arousing and situating the human[3] would be dedicated to
caretaking or illuminating or obscuring or forgetting Being [*l'être*],
which is not in the being [*étant*]. Subjectivity would appear, in view

of its own disappearance, as a moment necessary to the manifestation of the structure of Being, of the Idea. A moment almost in the temporal sense of momentary, transitory, passing, even if a whole history and a whole civilization is drawn in its passage. Yet this passage does not constitute a new dimension. Studied by structuralist anthropology as a reality itself made of structures, it belongs to an objective order that this anthropology only sets up and to which it is no exception.

Subjectivity, the setting up of intelligible structures, would have no internal finality. We would witness the ruin of the myth of man as end in himself, giving way to the appearance of an order that is neither human nor inhuman, ordained of course through man and the civilizations he produces, but ordaining itself, in the last analysis, by the appropriately rational force of the dialectical or logico-formal system. A non-human order, suited to the name that is anonymity itself: matter.[4]

To find man in that matter and a name in that anonymity—a being in that lunar landscape—must we not give value to the "transcendentals": *something* or *the One*? Against the universality of structures and the impersonal essence of being—against the reciprocal relativity of points in a system—there has to be a point that counts for itself, and in the "Bacchic delirium when no limb escapes from drunkenness," there needs to be a cell that is in itself sober. From the upsurge of *the being* in the matrix of *something* or on the model of *the One* in the heart of *Being*—that is, in the heart of what is called the *Being of the being*— would hang the essence of man. But we can also see the danger of such a demand: a return to the philosophy of substance, of material support, the thingification of man, whereas it was a matter of rendering him the utmost dignity. How do *the one* and *the unique* arise in essence? Seeking the matrix of the being in *pleasure* or the *present*, in the marvelous instant worthy of lasting or, more exactly, in time reposing in its hour, in happiness; countering the universality of reason, which is not a being, with the emotional resources hidden in the body and heart of man, means remaining attached to the idea of repose that suggests substance as the material support. Which gives us the being torn out of the anonymity of Being, falling and dissolving into nature.[5] The *rational animal* as *animal* blends into nature; as *rational* it pales in the light where it brings to manifestation the Ideas, concepts returned to themselves, logical and mathematical sequences, structures.

2

The inefficacy of human action teaches us how precarious is the concept "man." But to think human action on the level of labor and commandment is to approach it in its derivative forms. An action that is distinct from a simple repercussion of energy along a causal chain is the fact of *beginning,* of *existing* as origin and from an origin toward the future. It is then accomplished in the free inchoative—principled—character of *consciousness.* Consciousness is a mode of being such that beginning is its *essential.* To begin—to ignore or suspend the undefined density of the past—is the wonder of the *present.* All contents of consciousness were received, were present and consequently are present or represented, memorable. Consciousness is the very impossibility of a past that had never been present, that is closed to memory and history. Action, freedom, beginning, present, representation—memory and history—articulate in various ways the ontological modality that is consciousness. Nothing can enter fraudulently as a sort of contraband into a conscious ego without being exposed to avowal, without its equivalent in avowal, without making itself truth. Therefore, all rationality comes down to discovery of the origin, the principle. Reason is an archaeology, and the composite word *archaeology* is redundant. The intelligibility of the subject itself can only be this return to the origin, a movement that, according to *Wissenschaftslehre,* is the very being of the Ego, the "posing oneself" of the oneself. The reflexivity of the Ego is nothing other than the fact of being the origin of the origin.

But already in the infinite adjournment of the *Sollen,* which flows from the subject posed as Ego, origin of self or liberty, is announced the failure included in the human act and arises the anti-humanism that will reduce man to a milieu necessary to being so it can reflect itself and show itself in its truth, that is, in the systematic lineup of concepts. So then we may wonder: couldn't humanism take on some sense if we thought through to the very limit the denial that being inflicts on freedom? Couldn't a sense be found (sense "on the wrong side," of course, but the only authentic sense here) to liberty itself, going from the very passivity of the human where its inconsistency seems to appear? Couldn't this sense be found without getting pushed to the "Being of the being," to system, to matter?

It would mean a new concept of passivity, a passivity more radical than that of effect in a causal series, *beneath* consciousness and knowledge, but also *beneath* the inertia of things reposing on itself as substances and opposing their nature, material cause, to all activity; it would mean a passivity referred to the *wrong side* of being, prior to the ontological plane where being is posed as *nature,* referred to the anteriority of creation, not yet having an outside, to meta-physical anteriority. As if beyond the *ambit* of a melody a higher or lower register resonated and mixed with the chords that are heard, but with a sonority that no voice can sing and no instrument can produce.[6] Pre-original anteriority that could of course be called religious, if the term didn't carry the risk of a theology impatient to recuperate "spiritualism": present, representation and principles, precisely excluding the "beneath."

To revive the inanity of the man-principle, the inanity of the Principle, doubts about freedom understood as origin and present, to seek subjectivity in radical passivity—is this not surrender to the fatality or determination that is the very abolition of the subject? Yes, if the alternative free/not free is ultimate, and subjectivity means stopping at the ultimate or the original. But this is precisely the point of our interrogation. Undoubtedly the Ego in its isolation, in the apparently absolute separation of the psyche and the sovereign liberty of representation, knows nothing beneath its freedom or outside the necessity that comes up against that freedom but is presented to it. It must, as Fichte argues, be its own source. It is absent from its birth and death, with no father and no murderer, and sentenced to give them to itself—to deduce them—deduce the non-ego from its liberty, at the risk of sinking into madness. The return to the ultimate or the original, to the principle, is already accomplished through the freedom of the Ego, which is the very beginning. The thesis and antithesis of the third Kantian antinomy imply the priority of the thesis, because the situation is not limited to themes: thesis and antithesis are presented to the consciousness which thematizes them and represents them to itself in the identity of the *said*, the logos,[7] one and the other offered to a freedom for acceptance or refusal. Absolute non-freedom absolutely could not show itself. But the ego can be put in question by Others in an exceptional way. Not as by an obstacle that it can always measure, or by death that it can also give to itself;[8] the Ego can be accused despite its innocence, by violence of course, but also, despite the separation where it is left by the exclusivism and insularity of the psychic, by Others who as such nevertheless "obsess" it and who, near or distant, impute to it a responsibility, unimpugnable as a traumatism, a responsibility for which it made no decision but cannot escape, enclosed in self. Reduced to silence it still gives a response from beneath the logos, as if its voice had a range of low or high notes beyond the low and high. Indeclinable subject, precisely as irreplaceable *hostage* of others, prior to the amphibology of Being and being, and to the condition of a nature.[9]

So one can speak of a "beyond the ultimate" or "pre-original" without their becoming, by that beyond or beneath, ultimate or original. The "beneath" or "pre-originary" or "pre-liminary" designates—by an abuse of language of course—this subjectivity prior to the Ego, prior to its freedom and non-freedom. Pre-original subject, outside of being, *in self. Interiority* is not described here in spatial terms as the volume of a sphere enveloped and sealed to Others but that, formed like consciousness, would also be reflected in the Said and thus belong to the space common to all, to the synchronic order, even if it had to be part of the most secret region of this sphere. *Interiority is the fact that in being* the beginning is preceded but that which precedes is not presented to the free gaze that would assume it, does not make itself present or representation; something already happened "over the head" of the present, did not pass through the cord of consciousness and does not let itself be recuperated; something that precedes the beginning and the principle, something that is, an-archically, *despite* being, reverses or precedes being. But is it really a *something*? The something resides *in* being, assumable and exterior. Here we are talking about an unassumable passivity that does not *name* itself or names itself only by abuse of language, pro-noun of subjectivity. The right side of being includes a wrong side that cannot turn inside out. But this expression is not the result of some kind of complacency for the unutterable and in-communicable. The unutterable or incommunicable of interiority that cannot hold in a Said is a responsibility prior to freedom. The un-speakability of the unutterable is described by the preoriginality of responsibility for others, by a responsibility prior to all free engage-ment, before describing itself by its inability to appear in the *said*.[10] Therefore, the subject does not clash with being by a freedom that would make it master of things but by a preoriginary susceptibility[11] more ancient than the origin, a susceptibility provoked in the subject,[12] where the provocation is never made present or logos offered for as-sumption or refusal and placed in the bipolar field of values. Through this susceptibility the subject is responsible for his responsibility, un-able to escape from it without keeping a trace of his desertion.[13] It is responsibility before being intentionality.

3

But isn't this servitude? *Not being able* to get out of responsibility? How can this passivity place the subject "beyond freedom and non-free-dom"? How is the susceptibility of pre-originary responsibility prior to confrontation with the logos, to its presence, prior to the beginning that is presented (or presentified) to the agreement one grants or re-fuses to the logos, how is this not enslavement? Why does the subject, banished in self, held at bay by responsibility, brought back to its irre-placeable unicity by this irrefusable responsibility, exalt in the irrefus-ability of the One?

If determination by the Other is to be called servitude the determined must remain *other* with regard to that which determines it. In fact, true and simple determinism is not servitude for any of the terms that con-stitute the unity of an order. If the determined is to be other with regard to that which determines it, however, it has to be free; it must keep a memory of the present when the determining determined it and was its contemporary. This power of reminiscence is precisely what escaped determination, the part—be it infinitesimal—of freedom necessary for the condition of servitude. Absolute passivity, where the determining term was never presented to the determined, not even in memory, is equivalent to determinism. Is determinism beyond freedom and servitude? Certainly. But subjectivity is beneath the determinism-servitude alternative. The rendezvous of presentation of the determinant to the determined, to which one would want to carry the origin of responsibility, may have been impossible if the determinant is the Good, which is not the object of a choice because it is seized by the subject before the subject has had the time—that is, the distance—necessary for choice. There is no enslavement more complete than this seizure by the good, this election. But the enslaving character of responsibility that overflows choice—of obedience prior to the presentation or representation of the commandment that obliges to responsibility— is canceled by the bounty of the Good that commands.[14] Beneath enslavement the obedient finds his integrity. Irrefusable responsibility nonetheless never assumed in complete freedom, is *good*. The seizure by the good, the passivity of "enduring the good," is a more profound contraction than moving the lips in imitation of that contraction to articulate the *yes*. Here ethics makes its entry into the philosophic discourse—rigorously ontological at the start—as an extreme reversal of its possibilities. Starting from a radical passivity of subjectivity it reached the notion of "a responsibility overflowing freedom" (whereas only freedom should be able to justify and limit responsibilities), an obedience prior to the reception of orders; from this anarchic situation of responsibility, the analysis—undoubtedly by abuse of language— named the Good.

To be dominated by the Good does not mean choosing the Good from a position of neutrality in the face of an axiologic bipolarity. The concept of such a bipolarity already refers to freedom, to the absolute of the present, and would mean the impossibility of going beneath the *principle* to the absolute of knowledge. However, to be dominated by the Good is precisely to exclude for oneself the very possibility of choice, of coexistence in the present. Here the impossibility of choice is not the result of violence—fatalism or determinism—it is unimpugnable election by the Good that, for the elected, is always already accomplished. Election by the Good that is, precisely, not *action;* it is non-violence itself. Election meaning nomination of the non-interchangeable. Whence passivity more passive than all passivity, filial, but pre-liminary pre-log-

ical subjection, subjection to a unique sense that it would be wrong to
understand as coming from a dialogue. The passivity, unconvertible into
present, is not a simple *effect* of a Good which would be reconstructed
as cause of this effect; the Good *is* in this passivity, the Good that strictly
speaking doesn't have to *be* and *is* not, except by bounty. The passivity
is the being of the *beyond being* of the Good, which language rightfully
circumscribes—as usual by betraying—with the word *non-being;* passivity is the place [*lieu*]—or more exactly the no place [*non-lieu*]—of the
Good, its exception to the rule of being, ever unveiled in the logos, its exception to the present.[15] Plato recalls the long travails of the eye that tries
to fix the sun in its sojourn. But the sun is not forever removed from
the gaze. The invisible of the Bible is the idea of the Good beyond being.
To be obliged to responsibility has no beginning. Not in the sense of
some sort of perpetuity or of a perpetuity that would claim to be eternity (which is probably the extrapolation that gives "bad infinity") but
the sense of an inconvertibility into an assumable present. A notion that
is not purely negative. It is responsibility overflowing liberty, that is, responsibility for others. It is the trace of a past that refuses itself to the
present and to representation, the trace of an immemorial past.

It is by the Good that the obligation to responsibility—irrevocable,
irreversible, unimpugnable but not going back to a choice—is not a violence that would collide with a choice; it situates an "interiority" preceding freedom and non-freedom, outside axiologic bipolarity, an obedience to a unique value without anti-value, that is inescapable[16] but
that, "related" to the subject, is neither chosen nor non-chosen, and
where the subject is elected, and keeps the trace of election. A value
never offered as theme, not present, not represented and that, so as not
to be thematized, not begin, is more antique than the principle and,
in an immemorial past without present, by the ambiguity and the an-
tiquity of the trace, non-absent. A value that, by abuse of language, is
named. A value that is named God. Thematization would turn the pre-
original passivity of the elected submitting to election into choice made
by the subject, and would turn subjectivity—or subjection—into
usurpation. The subjectivity of the in-itself is like obedience to an order
accomplished before the order makes itself heard: anarchy itself. The
subject as Ego stands already in freedom, beyond self, beyond the re-

lation to the pre-original, the pre-liminary, beyond pure passivity more ancient than that which, its <u>inertia *colliding with* activity</u>, supposes it. Pure passivity preceding freedom is responsibility. But the responsibility that owes nothing to my freedom is my responsibility for the freedom of others. There where I could have remained spectator, I am responsible, that is to say again, speaking. Nothing is theater anymore, the drama is no longer a game. Everything is serious.[17]

4

But nothing in the passivity of possession by the Good where the Good *is*—whereas *strictly speaking* it doesn't have to be and is not unless by bounty—becomes a natural tendency. The relation with the Other is not converted into nature or promise of happiness enfolding this relation with the Other in happiness. *The passivity where the Good is, is not made Eros;* nothing in this passivity suppresses the trace of the Other in his virility to bring Other back to Same. The anarchic bond between the subject and the Good—a bond that cannot be tied as assumption of a principle that by whatever rights would be present to the subject in choice, but rather an anarchic bond tied without the subject being will—is not the constitution of a "divine instinct" of responsibility, an "altruistic or generous nature," a "natural bounty." It ties up with an outside. This exteriority of the covenant is maintained precisely in the effort demanded by responsibility for others, foreign to Eros as to enthusiasm (possession where the difference between possessing and possessed disappears). But it needs the temptation of the facility of rupture, the erotic attraction of irresponsibility that, through a responsibility limited by the freedom of he "who is not his brother's keeper," portends the Evil of the absolute freedom of play. Whence comes the seduction of irresponsibility in the heart of submission to the Good, the probability of egoism in the subject responsible for his responsibility, that is to say the very birth of the Ego in obedient will. This temptation to separate from the Good is the very embodiment of the subject[18] or its presence in being. But it is not because the Ego is an embodied soul that temptation disturbs the obedience preliminary to the Good and promises man the sovereign choice; it is because obedience without servitude to the Good is obedience to an *other* remaining other, that the subject is carnal, on the edge of Eros, and makes itself being.

The essence of Evil is its insurmountable ambiguity. It may be that easy seductive evil cannot rupture the passivity of the pre-liminary pre-historic subjection, annihilate the beneath, repudiate what the subject never contracted. Evil shows itself as sin, that is, responsibility in spite of itself for refusing responsibilities. Neither beside nor facing Good, but in second place, under, lower than Good. Being persevering in being, egoism or Evil, designates the very dimension of lowliness and the birth of hierarchy. That is where axiologic bipolarity begins. But Evil claims to be a contemporary, an equal, the twin brother of Good. Irrefutable lie, Luciferian lie. Without he who is the very egoism of the Ego posing as its own origin—uncreated—sovereign principle, prince, without the im-possibility of climbing down from this pride, the anarchic submission to Good would not be an-archic anymore, it would be equivalent to the demonstration of God, to theology treating God as if he belonged to being or to perception, it would be equivalent to the optimism that the-ology can teach and religion must hope for, but philosophy must not speak. This silence can be taken for the dissolving of man in being that tempts him and where he enters. Modern anti-humanism is undoubt-edly right in not finding in man taken as individual of a genus or an on-tological reason—an individual like all substances persevering in be-ing—a privilege that makes him the aim of reality.

But the Ego brought down to Self, responsible in spite of itself, ab-rogates the egoism of the *conatus* and introduces sense into being. There can be no sense in being except for sense that is not measured by being. Death renders senseless all care the Ego would like to have for its existence and destiny. An enterprise with no outcome and al-ways ridiculous; nothing is more comical than the care for itself taken by a being doomed to destruction, which is just as absurd as ques-tioning, in view of action, the stars whose verdict cannot be appealed. Nothing is more comical or nothing is more tragic. It pertains to the same man to be tragic and comic. But the pre-original responsibility for the other is not measured by being, is not preceded by a decision, and cannot be reduced to absurdity by death. To pleasure, the only thing that can make us forget the tragicomedy of being and that may well be defined by this forgetting, death comes calling like a denial as it finishes off the sacrifice of unimpugnable responsibility. No one, not even the promisers of religion, is hypocritical enough to claim that he took away death's sting; but we may have responsibilities for which we must consent to death. The Other concerns me despite myself.

If one had the right to retain a single feature of a philosophic system while neglecting the details of its architecture—though there are no details in architecture, according to Valéry, and in philosophy it is the detail that keeps the ensemble from leaning—we would evoke Kant here: to find a sense to the human without measuring it by ontology, without knowing and without wondering "what about [qu'en *est*-il de] . . . ," outside mortality and immortality—this may well be the Copernican revolution.

From a responsibility even more ancient than the *conatus* of substance, more ancient than the beginning and the principle, from the anarchic, the ego returned to self, responsible for Others, hostage of everyone, that is, substituted for everyone by its very non-interchangeability, hostage of all the others who, precisely *others,* do not belong to the same genus as the ego because I am responsible for them without concerning myself about their responsibility for me because I am, in the last analysis and from the start, even responsible for that, the ego, I; I am man holding up the universe "full of all things." Responsibility or saying prior to Being and beings, not saying itself in ontological categories. Modern anti-humanism may be wrong in not finding for man, lost in history and in order, the trace of this pre-historic an-archic saying.

⚘ ⚘ ⚘ Without Identity

> If I don't answer for myself, who will answer for me?
> If I answer only for myself—am I still myself?
> —Babylonian Talmud, Tractate Avot 6a

1. The Social Sciences

The end of humanism, end of metaphysics, the death of man, death of God (or death to God!): apocalyptic ideas or intellectual high-society slogans. Typical of such manifestations of Parisian taste, and distaste, these notions take hold with the tyranny of the latest craze, but are soon reduced to bargain prices and downgraded.

Their primary truth is methodological. They express a certain state of research in the social sciences. A concern for rigor makes psychologists, sociologists, historians, and linguists mistrustful of an Ego that listens to itself, questions itself, but remains defenseless against the illusions of its class and the fantasies of its latent neurosis. A formalism is required to tame the wild proliferation of human facts that, broached in their contents, blur the theoretician's vision, and to measure the certitude of knowledge, which is more assured of the limits of its axiomatics than of any given axiom. The study of man involved in a civilization and economy that have become worldwide cannot be confined to a dawning of awareness: henceforth his death, renaissance, and transformation are played out far from himself. Whence the aversion to a preachiness that befell Western humanism—despite its past science and audacity—establishing in the remarkable ambiguity of *lofty literature* "lofty spirits" with no hold on the realities of violence and exploitation. All respect for the "human mystery" is thereafter denounced as ignorance and oppression. "To nobly say the human in man, to think the humanity in man, is to quickly arrive at a discourse that is untenable

and, how can it be denied, more repugnant than all the nihilist vulgar-
ities," wrote Maurice Blanchot in November 1967.[1]

Taking principles of method for affirmations on the foundation of
things (if one may still really speak of the foundation of things after
the end of metaphysics) is certainly an act of hasty simple minds.

The fact remains that the social sciences are thriving in our times
because of a mutation of the light of the world, the preemption of certain significations. A nostalgia for logical formalism and mathematical structures for understanding man overflows methodological pre-
cautions and magic tricks, and surpasses the positivist imitation of
triumphant archetypes of number and measure in physics. It is a clear
preference, all the way into the human order, for mathematical identities identifiable from the outside as against the coincidence of self
with self where attempts were still being made a hundred years ago to
anchor the ship of exact knowledge. *Henceforth the subject is eliminated
from the order of reasons.* As if even its congruence with self were impossible; as if the interiority of the subject were not closed from the inside. The psyche and its liberties (where nevertheless the scholar's own
exploratory thought unfolds) would be but a detour taken by structures in order to link up in a system and bring themselves to light. It
is no longer man with his own vocation who would seek or posses the
truth, it is the truth that arouses and holds man (without holding to
him!). The interiority of an ego identical to itself dissolves in a totality without folds or secrets. All that is human is outside. This can pass
for a very firm formulation of materialism.

Anyway, where in being without issue can a no-man's-land be found
for the fallback of transcendental subjectivity? In recalling the vener-
able reasons that "transcendental consciousness" imposes on philosophy trying to understand knowledge [*connaissance*], one might of
course have persisted in thinking being in function of subjectivity and
a "no place" where the legislative sovereignty of transcendental consciousness would stand. But isn't the identity of the subjective ruined
by the contradictions that tear apart this reasonable world, supposedly
resulting from transcendental legislation? That an action can be ham-
pered by the technique destined to make it easy and effective, that a science born to embrace the world delivers it to disintegration, that pol-

itics and an administration guided by the humanist ideal maintain the exploitation of man by man, and war—these are singular reversals of reasonable projects; they disqualify human causality and, thereby, transcendental subjectivity understood as spontaneity and act. It is as if the Ego, identity par excellence where all identifiable identity is derived, defaulted on itself, could not coincide with itself.

Of course men have been sensitive to this alienation for a long time. But since the nineteenth century, with Hegel, a sense was found to this alienation, recognized as transitory and supposed to bring a surplus of consciousness and clarity to the fulfillment of things. Those sidesteps of will were explained, especially in Marx, by social alienation; in the exaltation of socialist hopes, transcendental idealism was paradoxically rendered plausible! Today's angst is more profound. It comes from seeing revolutions founder in bureaucracy and repression and totalitarian violence passing for revolution. *Because disalienation itself is alienated in them.* In the revolutionary enterprise led with an extreme consciousness that nevertheless undoes the vigilant intention that desires it, in action ripped out of the firm hand—the iron fist—that guides it, fails or at least is denounced the *recurrence to self,* the idea of an ego that is identified in finding itself. The reunion of self and self is a flop. Interiority is not rigorously interior. *I is an other.* Is not identity itself a failure? Sense would be sought in a world that bears no human traces and is not falsified by the identity of significations. In a world pure of all ideology.

2. Heidegger

There is a significant convergence in contemporary thought between doubts on subjectivity in the social sciences and the most influential philosophic thought of our century, which already tries to be post-philosophic.[2] Heidegger attaches the notion of transcendental subjectivity to a certain orientation in European philosophy, to metaphysics. He thinks this metaphysics is ending. Irreducible identity, Ego, psyche, consciousness, subject, the possibility of confining oneself in self and separating oneself from being, of going thence to being from this fall-back in self (which in modern thought is the certainty of self, for which the Cartesian cogito set the model)—all of that would still be metaphysics. The same would hold for the idea that the cultural, political, or technical act would project the rays of its inner light, source of sense, into the abstruseness of Being, and cover opaque being with layers of sense in the course of history that would be the movement of reason itself, transfiguring Being by Art, Science, Government, and Industry. For Heidegger the very process of being, the *essence* of being,[3] is the emergence of a certain sense, a certain light, a certain peace that borrows nothing from the subject, expresses nothing that is interior to a soul. The process of being, or the *essence* of being, is forthwith manifestation, that is, flourishing on site, in world, in hospitality. But then the manifestation needs man, because it confides in man as secret and as task. Confidant but also speaker, harbinger, messenger of being, man does not express any deep interior. Standing in the opening of being, whose essence is patency, man says being. In the opening, but also in the forgetting! In the "forgetting of being" man is confined like a monad; he makes himself soul, consciousness, psychic life. From that closure, where Being still interprets, understands, and shows itself, but unbeknownst to the soul, which only pronounces being, the European metaphysics that is ending expressed history. But it is ending. The "deep inside" is no longer a world. *The inner world is contested by Heidegger as by the social sciences.* To think, after the end of metaphysics, is to reply to the silent language of the invitation, reply from the depth of listening to the peace that is the original language, marvel at this silence and this space. Simplicity and wonder that are also the endurance and extreme attention of poets and artists; it is, in the proper meaning of the term, keeping the silence, tending the silence. The poem or work of art tends the silence, *lets the essence of being be,* like the shepherd tends his flock. *Being needs man just as a fatherland or a soil needs natives.* The strangeness of man to the world, this stateless condition, would attest the last shudders of metaphysics and the humanism it upholds. By this denunciation of the "inner world," Heidegger radicalizes Husserl's anti-psychologism.[4] The end of subjectivity began with the twentieth century. The social sciences and Heidegger lead to the triumph of mathematical intelligibility, sending the subject, the individual, his unicity and his election back into ideology, or else rooting man in being, making him its messenger and poet.

3. Subjectivity and Vulnerability

Now it is time to ask some questions. Does human causality accord with the sense of subjectivity? Does the Act—intervention in Being founded on the representation of Being, that is, founded on consciousness where Being is presented and thus always collects itself, present and represented, and comes back in reminiscence "to its beginnings" and thus indulges in freedom, always correlative to an intentionality—the free Act assuming that which imposes on me, remaining, even in the face of the ineluctable, will, good face to bad game, activity resurging under the passivity of impression—does the free Act respond to the vocation of subjectivity? Can't subjectivity relate to—without representing it to itself—a past that passes all present and thus overflows the measure of freedom? This would be a relation prior to the understanding of a vocation, preceding understanding and unveiling, preceding the truth. Well, in the approach to others, where others are from the start under my responsibility, "something" has overflowed my freely made decisions, has slipped into me *unbeknownst to me,* alienating my identity. Is it then certain that in the deportation or drift of identity perceived through the reversal of human projects the subject did not signify with all its youthful radiance? Is it certain that Rimbaud's "I is another" means only alteration, alienation, betrayal of self, strangeness of self, and servitude to that stranger? Is it certain that the most humble experience of the one who *puts himself in the other's place,* that is, accuses himself of the other's illness or pain, is not already animated by the most eminent sense in which "I is another"?

All that is human is outside, say the social sciences. It is all outside and everything in me is open. Is it certain that subjectivity, in this exposure to all winds, is lost among things or in matter? Doesn't subjectivity signify precisely by its incapacity to shut itself up from inside? Opening can in fact be understood in several senses.

First it can signify the opening of all objects to all others, in the unity of the universe governed by the third analogy of experience in *Critique of Pure Reason.*

But the term *opening* can designate the intentionality of consciousness, an ecstasy in being. Ecstasy of ex-sistence, according to Heidegger, animating consciousness that, by the original opening of the *essence* of being (*Sein*), is called to play a role in this drama of opening. Drama of which ex-sistence would also be the vision or speculation. The ecstasy of intentionality would then be founded in the truth of being, in parousia. Didn't naturalism foresee this mode of foundation by positing consciousness as avatar of nature? Avatar and thence, in its extraneousness with regard to being, its exception, epiphenomenon.

However, *opening* can have a third sense. No longer the essence of being that opens to show itself, not consciousness that opens to the presence of the essence open and confided in it. Opening is the stripping of the skin exposed to wound and outrage. Opening is the vulnerability of a skin offered in wound and outrage beyond all that can show itself, beyond all that of essence of being can expose itself to understanding and celebration. In sensibility "is uncovered," is exposed a nude more naked than the naked of skin that, form and beauty, inspires the plastic arts; nakedness of a skin offered to contact, to the caress that always, even ambiguously in voluptuousness, is suffering for the suffering of the other. Uncovered, open like a city declared open to the approaching enemy, sensibility beneath all will, all act, all declaration, all taking stands—is vulnerability itself. *Is* it? Doesn't its being consist in divesting itself of being; not to die, but to alter into "otherwise than being"? Subjectivity of the subject, radical passivity of man who elsewhere poses himself, declares himself being and considers his sensibility an attribute. Passivity more passive than all passivity, sent back into the pronominal particle *se*, which has no nominative. The Ego from top to toe and to the very marrow is—vulnerability.

"Opening" of the sensibility cannot be interpreted as simple exposure to the affection of causes. The other *by whom* I suffer is not simply the "stimulus" of experimental psychology and not even a cause that, by the intentionality of suffering, would by whatever rights be thematized. Vulnerability is more (or less) than passivity receiving form or shock. It is the aptitude—that any being in its "natural pride" would be ashamed to admit—for "being beaten," for "getting slapped." As admirably expressed in a prophetic text:[5] "He turns his cheek to the one who slaps him and is satiated with shame." Without introducing any deliberate seeking of suffering or humiliation (turning the other cheek)

it suggests, in the primary suffering, in suffering as suffering, a hard unbearable consent that animates passivity, strangely animates it in spite
of itself, whereas passivity as such has neither force nor intention, neither like it or not. The impotence or humility of "to suffer" is beneath
the passivity of submission. Here the word *sincerity* takes all its sense:
to discover oneself totally defenseless, to be surrendered. Intellectual
sincerity, veracity, already refers to vulnerability, is founded in it.

Thus, in vulnerability lies a *relation to the other* that is not exhausted
by causality, a relation prior to all affection by the stimulus. The identity of the *self* does not set limits to submission, not even the last resistance that matter "in potential" opposes to the form that invests it. Vulnerability is obsession by others or approach to others. It is *for others,*
from behind the *other* of the stimulus. An approach reduced neither to
representation of others nor to consciousness of proximity. To suffer by
the other is to take care of him, bear him, be in his place, consume oneself by him. All love or hatred of one's fellow man as a thoughtful attitude supposes this prior vulnerability, this "moaning of the entrails[6]"
mercy.[7] From the moment of sensibility, the subject is *for the other:* substitution, responsibility, expiation. But a responsibility that I did not assume at any moment, in any present. Nothing is more passive than this
challenge prior to my freedom, this pre-original challenge, this sincerity. Passivity of the vulnerable, condition (or incondition) by which being
shows itself creature.

Sincerity exposes—unto wounding. The active Ego returns to the passivity of a *self,* to the accusative of the *se* that is derived from no nominative, to the accusation prior to any misdeed.[8] But exposure never passive enough: exposure exposes itself, sincerity bares sincerity itself. There
is saying. As if saying had sense prior to the truth that it unveils, prior to
the advent of the knowledge and information it communicates, pure of
all said, saying that doesn't say a word, that infinitely—pre-voluntarily—
consents. Out in the open, in the sincerity where the veracity will come
long afterward to found itself, and thus outside of all thematic display, behold the subjectivity of the subject innocent of ontological conjunctions,
subjectivity of the subject from before *essence:* youth. But youth that does
not signify simply the incompletion of a future freshly broached, the possible calling essence. The youth philosophy loves—the "before being,"

"otherwise than being." Doesn't the modal thought of Jeanne Delhomme sight this difficult modality "without continuity with self, without continuation of self?" Marvelous moments: the One without being of Plato's *Parmenides;* the *I* that sticks up in the cogito when all being is shipwrecked but before the rescue of the *I* in being, as if the shipwreck never happened; the Kantian unity of the "I think" before its reduction to a logical form that Hegel would bring down to the concept; Husserl's pure Ego, transcendent in immanence, beneath the world, but also beneath the absolute being of reduced consciousness; the Nietzschean man shaking up the being of the world in the passage to the superman; "reducing" being, not by putting brackets here and there, but by the violence of an unheard-of verb, undoing by the non-saying of dance and laughter (why, we don't know, tragic and grave and on the brink of madness) the worlds that weave the aphoristic verb that demolishes them; retiring from the time of aging (of passive synthesis) by the thought of the eternal return. Phenomenological reduction seeking the pure Ego beyond being could not be obtained by the effect of writing when the ink of the world stains the fingers that put this world in brackets.

But the philosopher has to come back to language to translate—be it by betraying them—the pure and unspeakable.

4. Strangeness to Being

Let us finally dare to ask some questions about Heidegger. Is man's strangeness to the world the effect of a process that began with the pre-Socratics saying the opening of being without preventing the oblivion of that opening through Plato, Aristotle, and Descartes? The soul exiled in this world, transmitted by Plato to metaphysical thought, already attests the oblivion of being. But does the notion of the subject reflect solely what Heidegger calls the history of being, whose eras are delineated by metaphysical oblivion in the history of philosophy? Does the crisis of interiority mark the end of this strangeness of the exception or exile of the subject and of man? Is this, for stateless man, the return to a fatherland on earth?

Are we not—we Occidentals from California to the Urals, nourished as much by the Bible as by the pre-Socratics—are we not strangers to

the world in a different way that owes nothing to the certainty of the
cogito which, since Descartes, would express the Being of beings? A
strangeness to the world that the end of metaphysics cannot dissipate.
Are we faced with the non-sense infiltrating in a world where man,
until then, was not simply the shepherd of being but chosen for himself? Or does the strange defeat or defection of identity confirm man's
election, mine, to serve, but the election of the Other for himself? Biblical verses do not function here as proof but as testimony of a tradition and an experience. Don't they have as much right as Hölderlin
and Trakl to be cited? The scope of the question is broader: do the Holy
Scriptures read and commented in the West incline the Greek writing
of philosophers, or are they only united teratologically? Does philos-
ophizing mean deciphering in a palimpsest a buried scripture?

We read in Psalm 119[:19], "I am a stranger on the earth; do not hide
your commandments from me." Is this, as historical criticism claims,
a later text from the Hellenistic period when oriental spirituality may
have been seduced by the Platonic myth of the soul exiled in the body?
But this psalm echoes texts recognized as dating from one century before Socrates and Plato, notably in Leviticus chapter 25, verse 23: "No
land will be alienated irrevocably, because the land is mine, because you
are but strangers, housed in my land." This has nothing to do with the
strangeness of the eternal soul exiled amidst passing shadows, or the
homesickness that can be surmounted by the edification of a house and
possession of land, releasing by construction the hospitality of the site
that the land envelops. Because, as in psalm 119, which calls for commandments, this difference between the ego and the world is extended
by obligations toward others. Echo of the permanent *saying* of the Bible:
the condition—or incondition—of strangers and slaves in the land of
Egypt brings man closer to his fellow man. Men seek one another in
their incondition of strangers. No one is at home. The memory of that
servitude assembles humanity. The difference that gapes between ego
and self, the non-coincidence of the identical, is a thorough non-
indifference with regard to men.

The free man is dedicated to his fellow; no one can save himself without others. The inside-out domain of the soul does not close from inside. A text in Genesis [7:16] says with admirable precision that it is "the

Eternal who closed the door of the ark on Noah." How could it be closed at the hour when humanity was perishing? Are there hours when the deluge does not threaten? Behold the impossible interiority that disorients and reorients the social sciences in our times. An impossibility that we learn neither from metaphysics nor the end of metaphysics. The gap between ego and self, impossible recurrence, impossible identity. No one can stay in himself; the humanity of man, subjectivity, is a responsibility for others, an extreme vulnerability. The return to self becomes interminable detour. Prior to consciousness and choice, before the creature collects himself in present and representation to make himself essence, man approaches man. He is stitched of responsibilities. Through them, he lacerates essence. It is not a matter of a subject assuming responsibilities or avoiding responsibilities, not a subject constituted, posed in itself and for itself like a free identity. It is a matter of the subjectivity of the subject, his non-indifference to others in limitless responsibility, limitless because it is not measured by commitments going back to assumption and refusal of responsibilities. It is about responsibility for others, where the movement of recurrence is diverted to others in the "moved entrails" of the subjectivity it tears apart.

Foreign to self, obsessed by others, un-quiet, the Ego is hostage, hostage in its very recurrence of an ego endlessly failing to itself. And thus always closer to others, more obliged, aggravating its failure to self. This liability is resorbed only by enlargement; glory of non-essence! Passivity that no "healthy" will can wish for, and thus banished, separated, without gathering the merit of its virtues and talents, unable to collect itself so as to accumulate itself and swell with being. Non-essence of man, possibly less than nothing. "It may be," writes Blanchot, "as one likes to declare, that man passes." He passes, he even has already passed, to the extent that he was always appropriated to his own disappearance . . . So there's no need to deny humanism as long as we recognize it there where it receives its least deceiving mode, never in the zones of interiority of power and law, order, culture, heroic magnificence . . .

Without repose in self, without a solid base in the world, in that strangeness to all places, on the other side of being, beyond being—yes, that is some sort of interiority! It is not a philosopher's construction; it is the unreal reality of men persecuted in the everyday history of the world, whose dignity and sense were never retained in metaphysics, a reality to which philosophers veil their faces.

But that responsibility endured beyond all passivity from which no one can unleash me in raising me up from my incapacity to close myself in, that responsibility from which the Ego cannot escape—the ego for which the other cannot substitute himself—designates the uniqueness of the irreplaceable. Uniqueness without interiority, ego without repose in self, hostage of everyone, diverted from self in every movement of its return to self—man without identity. Man understood as an individual of a genus or as a *being* situated in an ontological region, persevering in being like all substances, has no privilege that would establish him as the aim of reality. But man must also be thought from the responsibility more ancient than the *conatus* of substance or interior identification, thought from the responsibility that, always calling on the outside, precisely disturbs that interiority; man must be thought from self putting himself despite himself in the place of everyone, substituted for everyone because of his very non-interchangeability; man must be thought from the condition or incondition of hostage, hostage of all the others who, precisely others, do not belong to the same genre as me, because I am responsible for them without reposing in their responsibility to me which would allow them to substitute themselves for me, because even for their responsibility I am, in the last analysis and from the beginning, responsible. It is by this supplementary responsibility that subjectivity is not the Ego [*le Moi*], but me [*moi*].

5. Youth

Do these remarks pertain to "untimely considerations," despite the fact that their starting point is our contemporary intellectual situation? Were they not shocking with their outdated, idealist, humanist vocabulary? This is the perfect occasion to ask, in closing, if the aspirations of today's youth, despite the violence and irresponsibility in which these aspirations degenerate, can do without thought devoted to subjectivity defined from responsibility and against the notion of being.[9]

The idea of a subjectivity that can't close itself in—unto substitution—responsible for all the others and, consequently, the idea of the defense of man understood as defense of the man other than me, presides over what is called in our day the critique of humanism. This is a rejection of responsibility as paralyzed in "lofty literature" where the Saying brought down to the Said enters into conjunction with its own conditions, builds into its contexts and loses the youth of saying,[10] youth that is rupture of the context, cutting word, Nietzschean word, prophetic word, word that has no status in being but has nothing arbitrary, because it comes from sincerity, that is, the very responsibility for others. It is this limitless responsibility, not felt as a state of the soul, a mood, but *signifying* in the itself of self, subjectivity of the subject consuming itself like cinders covered with ashes (but suddenly bursting into the flames of a living torch)—it is this responsibility, searing wound of cruelties and desolation endured by others, that characterizes our era, no less than those cruelties and desolations themselves. Given that man has not finished counting for man, despite the formal mathematism of structures, the new reading of Marx, and psychoanalytic technique, does it signify that life is basically stupid and closed to the science it engenders and that the human beast, according to an expression of doubtful wisdom, is invariable?

The subject that we have surprised in the saying from before the said was qualified as young. This adjective indicates the surplus of sense over the being that carries it and claims to measure and restrain it. In the fulgurance of certain great moments of 1968, quickly extinguished by a language just as wordy and conformist as the one it was supposed to replace, youth consisted in contesting a world already denounced long ago. But the denunciation had become, a long time ago, literature and ready-made expressions. Certain voices or certain cries restored its proper, impugnable signification. The vague notion of authenticity, so oft abused, took precise meaning there. Youth is authenticity. But youth defined by the sincerity that is not the brutality of confession and the violence of the act but approach to others and a taking charge of one's fellow man that comes from human vulnerability. Youth that could find responsibilities under the thick layer of literature that releases from responsibility, youth—that can no longer be chided with "if youth only knew"[11]—stopped being the age of transition and passage ("youth must pass") and showed itself as the humanity of man.

Notes

Foreword

1. Hegel: *Science of Logic:* "It is one of the profoundest and truest insights to be found in the *Critique of Pure Reason* that the *unity* which constitutes the nature of the *Notion* is recognized as the *original synthetic* unity of *apperception,* as unity of the I think, or of self-consciousness" [trans. A. V. Miller (London: George Allen and Unwin, 1969), 584].

2. Kant, *Critique of Pure Reason,* B.151 [trans. Norman Kemp Smith (London: Macmillan, Ltd., 1929), 164].

3. Where would action be placed in the *logical* form of unity?

4. "'Forgive for pity's sake the offense of your brothers and their fault and the evil they have done.' Hearing these words, Joseph wept . . ." (Genesis 50:17).

Signification and Sense

The ideas set forth in this study were covered in lectures given at the Collège Philosophique in 1961, 1962, and 1963 and, in January 1963, at the Faculté Universitaire Saint-Louis in Brussels. The last section of this text was presented in another context on 12 May 1963 at a seminar at the Wijsgerig Gezelschap, in Louvain, and published under the title "La Trace de l'Autre" in the *Tijdscrift voor Filosofie* in September of the same year.

1. We draw attention to *La Veille* (Gallimard, 1963), an astute work by Roger Laporte, which also develops the "notion" of *He.*

Humanism and An-Archy

1. See M. Serres, "Analyse symbolique et méthode structurale," one of the most enlightening exposés of new directions in the current mutation in phi-

losophy (*Revue Philosophique de la France et de l'étranger* [October–December 1967]). This analysis is all the more astute considering that it is dated 1961.

2. Which would justify Sartre's position that all engagement and all *nonengagement* presume freedom.

3. The expression of this subordination of the subject to anonymous structures or being was formulated in Western thought long before the current crisis of humanism. For Hegel, the subject is the distance between the subject and predicate of the speculative proposition: "Since that first Subject [of the system] enters into the determinations themselves and is their soul, the second Subject, viz. the knowing 'I,' still finds in the Predicate what it thought it had finished with and got away from, and from which it hoped to return into itself; and, instead of being able to function as the determining agent in the movement of predication, arguing back and forth whether to attach this or that Predicate, it is really still occupied with the self of the content, having to remain associated with it, instead of being for itself" (Hegel, *Phenomenology of Spirit* [trans. A. V. Miller (Oxford: Oxford University Press, 1977), 37–38]). J.-F. Marquet presents a clear, incisive commentary on this text in an excellent article to which we refer: "Système et sujet chez Hegel et Schelling," in *Revue de Métaphysique et de Morale* 2 (1968).

4. On this point Husserlian phenomenology is radically opposed to all the philosophy that, for a large part, grew out of it. On this point Husserlian phenomenology remains thoroughly humanist. Subjectivity—irreducible to the purely logical transcendental conditions of the Marburg school and closely resembling the human psyche, even after phenomenological ἐποχή—is the Absolute. *Intentional implication* is affirmed against the mainsprings of systems: themes, horizons, memory, sedimentation of history awaiting reactivation in a living subjectivity. The subject is not a moment in a nonhuman or ideal order. Quite the contrary, objectivity, structure, thought sense—whatever can be grasped in the attitude sighting or "intuitioning" the object—is always abstract. The gaze of reflection *on* subjectivity is the only one that can grasp that which "thought wanted to get to." *Thought turned toward the object thinks, one could say, infinitely less of the object than it thinks of itself.* One may of course question Husserl on the *sense of being* of subjectivity. But this would suppose that the question of the "sense of being" is the ultimate and that questioning is a search for the ultimate. Going back to the concrete of historical subjectivity, to intention, may be an entirely different kind of questioning, *beyond the thematizable and the ultimate,* and this regardless of the paths Husserlian phenomenology did in fact follow.

5. This is certainly the major difficulty of Mikel Dufrenne's *Pour l'homme*

(Paris: Seuil, 1968), a work that shows as much talent as courage, where man is restored to his natural essence, his region in being, whereas the "impossibility" of speaking of man as the individual of a genus emerges perhaps most clearly from the critique of humanism. "Me" and "Others" for whom I am responsible—we are *different* precisely through this unilateral responsibility. I uphold all things and Others, but otherwise than in the image of a substance at rest under the accidents.

6. Is Nietzsche not the exceptional breath that can give resonance to that "beyond"?

7. See our study "Language and Proximity" [in Levinas, *Unforeseen History*, trans. Nidra Poller (Urbana: University of Illinois Press, forthcoming); Levinas, *Collected Philosophical Papers*, trans. Alphonso Lingis (Pittsburgh, Pa.: Duquesne University Press, 1998, 2000), 109–26].

8. Certainly in the "last quarter of a second" it comes against me, inordinate; but then the Other is already approaching. See *Totality and Infinity* [trans. Alphonso Lingis (Pittsburgh, Pa.: Duquesne University Press, 1969), 234–35].

9. See our article "La Substitution," *Revue Philosophique de Louvain* [3] (August 1968).

10. Responsibility, the "pre-original," is *Saying*. But responsibility—imprudent and risky *Saying*, communication of self that all information presupposes. Being beneath, the beneath of being—is *Saying*, forever baring oneself, exposing oneself, *turning the cheek*, which is expiation of the violence endured by the fault of others and where the present of that violence already refers to the pre-original. But this *Saying* of responsibility carries in its extravagance, its transcendence, the possibility and the necessity of weighing, of thought, of justice. See the end of our article "Substitution."

11. Beneath the still relative passivity of matter and the inertia of things.

12. Provoked *in* the subject—or susceptibility that delineates the very subjectivity of the subject.

13. Against Fichte and against Sartre, who think that everything that is in the subject, all the way to the subject itself, goes back to a position due to the subject itself. But Sartre spoke of the subject *condemned* to freedom. The sense of that condemnation is described in the following pages.

14. Cancellation that lies in "aggravating" the servitude by revealing to me the face of the Other and ordaining me to him, while liberating me from myself. We will not develop here this aspect of the problem of subjectivity, reserved for another study but already alluded to in our previously cited articles "Language and Proximity" and "Substitution."

15. The good must not be thought on the level of sentiment softening the.

violence of a responsibility that is not justified by a free act and pertaining to the "experience of responsibility." It is of itself passivity—when precisely it *is*.

16. "Where can I hide? Let us flee into the infernal night! But what am I saying? There my father holds the urn of doom," says Racine in *Phaedra* (act 4, scene 6), where the responsibility of responsibility is fatality. But the paternity of the Good is perceived in the possibility. According to the Bible, the Eternal says to Joshua, "I will not fail you or forsake you" (Joshua 1:5). The impossible divorce is here the supreme refuge.

17. It may be there, in the perspective of the pre-original, the opening of the unimpugnable responsibility for others, or the passivity of the good, that creation can be called ex nihilo: passivity that excludes even receptivity, because whatever in creation would be able to minimally assume the act—like matter assuming through its potentials the form that penetrates it—arises only after the creative act is accomplished. A thesis that has no power—or does not have the weakness—to connect with the dogmatic affirmation on creation. The notion of creation is not introduced here as an ontological concept in a reversion to the first cause of being starting from a given or in a reversion to the origin of time starting from the present—a procedure that, despite the Kantian antinomies, would have miraculously found an argument that reduces the antithesis to silence. Creation is not thought here as affirmation of a thesis that, in the theme, in the present, already supposes freedom, that is, the supposedly uncreated Ego contesting creation. The "creaturiality" of the subject cannot make itself representation of the creation. It is "for the Ego," supposedly uncreated, its banishment in *self* in the passivity of a responsibility overflowing freedom.

18. Embodiment—thoroughly erotic—is also the impossibility of escaping oneself, that is, running away from one's responsibilities. Thereby the illusory character of the rupture with submission is seen.

Without Identity

1. *La Nouvelle Revue Française* 179:820–21. And, prophetically, more than six months before May 1968, Blanchot sees the humanism of the cry and the "written cry," the *"graffiti on the walls,"* replacing literary humanism.

2. On this subject see the excellent work by Mikel Dufrenne, *Pour l'homme* (Paris: Seuil, 1968). See also *Revue Internationale de Philosophie* 85–86, notably the article by Louis Marain. It should be noted, however, that Heidegger himself ranges logistics, sociology, and psychology among the manifestations of

nihilism and the will to power that belong to finishing metaphysics. See *Zur Seinsfrage, Wegmarken,* 220; see also note 4 [to this essay].

3. This term is employed here as the abstract noun of the verb *to be.*

4. The anti-psychologism in Husserl's work was directed particularly against the "naturalization" of consciousness but preserved the sovereign interiority of the subject in transcendental idealism. Transcendental subjectivity founded all knowledge. The intentionality by which consciousness signified *opening* constituted itself as *contents* on the level of immanent time. Noeses, noemata, and intentional objects all constituted themselves, in the last analysis, in the interior of the consciousness certain of itself: no matter if only phenomenology, and only after the fact, can reactivate and make explicit the—initially clandestine—work of the constituting consciousness! Consciousness takes into account the universe, protected against all traumatic breaking in, *secura adversus deos.* Heidegger's anti-psychologism questions this origin of all sense in Ego. Not, of course, by subordinating being to logical structures (which for Heidegger are not language) or to a mathematical texture (which for him is not a text). And this is quite new, this anti-psychologism that is not logicist! But for Heidegger the subject has nothing interior to express. It is altogether thought from Being and the truth of Being. Our own interrogation is situated there: is subjectivity not sincerity—putting oneself out in the open, which is not a theoretical operation but an offering of self—*before* standing in the "opening of the truth," before "unveiling being."

5. *Lamentations* 3:30.

6. We have in mind here the biblical term *rakhamin,* translated as "mercy" but bearing a reference to the word for uterus, *rekhem;* it means mercy that is like an emotion from maternal entrails.

7. *Jeremiah* 31:20.

8. The notion of subjectivity proposed here consists neither in a conjunction of structures nor in a network of reflexes. It does not come down to the interiority of transcendental consciousness secured against all traumatism and, from the depth of its very receptivity, assuming the given. Subjectivity *signifies* by a passivity more passive than all passivity, more passive than matter, by its vulnerability, by its sensibility, by its nakedness more naked than nakedness, by the sincere stripping of that very nakedness making itself saying, by the saying of responsibility, by the substitution where responsibility is said to the utmost, by the accusative without nominative of self, by exposure to the *traumatism* of the gratuitous accusation, by expiation for Others. Traumatism staggering the ever-awake consciousness projected into resignation through a

night where, under the effect of traumatism, is operated the reversal of Me in Self [*Moi en Soi*]. Night of unconsciousness [*d'inconscient*, "irresponsibility"], surely. But, finding the interhuman drama and the unconscious beyond the vigilance of transcendental idealism and classical psychology, one might think that the interhuman drama of the subjective is more profound than the erotic drama, and the latter carries the former. Eròs supposes the face.

9. It is interesting to note the dominance, among the most imperative "sentiments" of May 1968, of the refusal of a humanity defined by its satisfaction, by its receipts and expenditures, and not by its vulnerability more passive than all passivity, its debt to the other. What was contested, beyond capitalism and exploitation, was their conditions: the individual taken as accumulation in being, by honors, titles, professional competence—ontological tumefaction weighing so heavily on others as to crush them, instituting a hierarchical society that maintains itself beyond the necessities of consumption and that no religious breath could make more egalitarian. Behind the capital in *having* weighed a capital in *being*.

10. Impossibility to speak, which may be the most undebatable experience of our times. We feel that discourse is unbearable solemnity, declamation, sermon, such that we can't speak or hear anything but the algorithmic discourse of science, the commonplace "give me a glass of water," without being disheartened, and we are tempted by violent discourse, already a cry, destructive of the said.

11. Do they have the powers attributed to them in the past when they were denied knowledge and skills? Because, unless one would renounce society and drown in the limitless responsibility for others all possibility of answering *in fact,* one can avoid neither the said, nor letters, nor lofty literature, nor understanding of being, nor philosophy. One cannot do without them if one holds to manifesting to thought—albeit in deforming it—the beyond of being itself. Manifestation at the cost of a betrayal, but necessary to the justice resigned to tradition, continuity, institutions, despite their very infidelity. Not caring in the least means flirting with nihilism.

Index

Absence, metaphor for, 10–11
Actuality: end of, 6; of presence, 3–4
Alienation, social sciences and, 59–60
Anarchy, ix
Anthropology: philosophy linked to, 37–38; subjectivity and, 48
Anti-humanism: of Nazis and Heidegger, xiv, xvi, xlii n. 22; rejection of, xxxvii–xxxviii; truth of being and, xix–xxiii, 46–48
Anti-Platonism, 18–20
Aristotle, 24, 65
art, as embodiment, 17
Authenticity, of youth, 69

Baudelaire, Charles-Pierre, 12
Beaufret, Jean, xvi, xxi
Being: beneath/pre-original of, 50–55, 74 n. 17; consciousness as mode of, 49–52; culture vs., x–xiv; ecstasy in, 62–63; elevation as ordaining, 36–37; essence of, 17, 22–23, 48–49, 61; indelibility of, 42–43; limits of, 7–8; modality of history of, 47; process of collection of, 14–16; self-preservation in, xxxiv; sense introduced into, 56–57; as source of meaning, xiii, xviii–xxi; strangeness to, 65–68; third person beyond, 40–42; for time after one's own time, 27–29; totality of, 13–14, 18–20, 30; truth of, xix–xxiii, 46–48; universal justice and, xxxvii–xxxviii; working vs. celebrating of, 21–22. See also Philosophy of being

Being-in-act, concept of, 3–7
Bergson, Henri-Louis: anti-Platonism of, 18, 20; on identification of reality, 21–22; mentioned, xxix, 14, 18
Bible, function of, 65–68
Blanchot, Maurice, 59, 67, 74 n. 1
Blum, Léon, 28
Brunschvicg, Léon, 37
Buber, Martin, xliv n. 67, 44

Cassirer, Ernst: background of, x; flight from Nazism, xiv; on Heidegger, xxi–xxv; on humanism, xvi; as influence, xxxvi–xxxvii; Levinas's differences from, xxviii, xxxi–xxxii; on origin of meaning, xxxv; on symbol, xxix–xxx. See also Cassirer-Heidegger debate; Philosophy of culture
Cassirer-Heidegger debate: culture vs. being in, x–xiv; Levinas on, xv; Levinas's allusions to, xxix–xxx; significance of, vii–viii, xxxvii; Third Reich and, xiv–xvi
Christianity, 27. See also God
Civilization: Cassirer on, xxiii–xxv; judgments of, 38
Cohen, Hermann, x, xv, xlii n. 19
Colonization, 37
Comprehension, concept of, 20. See also Understanding, syntheses of
Consciousness: challenge of, 32–33, 36; concept of, 3–4; intentionality of, 62–63; as mode of being, 49–52; moral responsibility and, xxxi; naturaliza-

Sociality, concept of, 29–30
Social sciences: dehumanization in, ix, 46–48; fads in, 58–59; interiority contested by, 60–62, 69; Levinas's criticism of, xxxii–xxxiii; subject manifested to, 5
Socrates, 65
Spinoza, Baruch, xxxiv
Structuralism: discourse on, xxvi; Levinas's criticism of, xxxii–xxxiii; as opponent, ix; on source of meaning, xviii; subjectivity and, 48. *See also* Other; Social sciences
Subject: being and, 5; beneath/pre-original of, 50–55, 74 n. 17; as condemned to freedom, 73 n. 13; elimination of, 59–61; good linked to, 55–57; subordination of, 47–48, 72 n. 3
Subjectivist relativism, 46–48
Subjectivity: as absolute, 72 n. 4; contestation of, 46–48; finitude of, xii; freedom and, xiii–xiv; Hegel on, 17; Heidegger on, xli n. 17; passivity and, 50–51, 75–76 n. 8; responsibility for other and, 53–55, 67–68; Sartre on, xvii; vulnerability and, 62–65. *See also* Transcendental subjectivity
Suffering: opening and, 63–64; of other, xxxiii–xxxv
Sugarman, Richard, xv
Symbol: contents of vs. saying of, xxx–xxxi, 68–69, 76 n. 10; Heidegger and Cassirer on, xxix–xxx; humans as source of, xiii–xiv, xxiv–xxv

Tarfon (rabbi), xxxviii
Thought: embodiment of, 16–17; signification and, 16, 19–20; turned toward object, 72 n. 4; work and, 26–27
Time: being for time after one's own, 27–29; impossibility of stopping, 34; insertion of space into, 42–43
Tolstoy, Leo, 36
Totality: of being, 13–14, 18–20, 30;

Levinas's work on, xxvi–xxvii, xxxviii; signification, cultural gesture, and, 13–17; work and, 26–27
Trace, face signified as, 41–44
Transcendence: immanence refused by, 40–42; of meaning, xxxv–xxxvi; of other, xxvi–xxviii, xxxv–xxxvi; of "saying" of responsibility, 69, 73 n. 10
Transcendental apperception: concept of, 4–5, 47; limits of, 6–7; of understanding, 15
Transcendental reduction: ego and, 4–5, 64–65; Husserl on, 4–5, 34, 47
Transcendental subjectivity: concept of, 4–5; elimination of, 59–61
Translations, xxxviii–xl, xlv–xlvi
Traumatism, subjectivity and, 75–76 n. 8. *See also* Suffering
Truth: of being, xix–xxiii, 46–48; generosity, dignity, and, 37; Levinas vs. Heidegger on, xxix–xxx; Plato on, 34–35; problem of, xi

Understanding, syntheses of, 15. *See also* Comprehension, concept of
Universality: direction of, 37–38
Univocality: freedom linked to, 26; loss of, 23–24

Valéry, Paul, xxxix, 29, 40, 57
Visage. See Face
Vision, by essence, 14–15. *See also* Face
Vulnerability, subjectivity and, 62–65

Weil, Eric, 26–27
Wirklichkeit, reality and, 21–22
Words, as references to other words, 11–12
Work: celebration vs., 21–22; sense and, 25–29
World (or horizon), signification situated in, 11
Wyschogrod, Edith, xxvi

Youth, philosophy and, 64–65

EMMANUEL LEVINAS (1906–95) is widely considered one of the most important continental philosophers of the twentieth century.

NIDRA POLLER is the translator of a number of works, including Ahmadou Kourouma's *Monnew* (Mercury House, 1992) and Michael Jeanneret's *Perpetual Motion* (Johns Hopkins University Press, 2001). A graduate of the University of Wisconsin and Johns Hopkins University, and a former faculty member at Federal City College (Washington, D.C.), she has lived in Paris since 1972.

RICHARD A. COHEN is the Isaac Swift Distinguished Professor of Judaic Studies at the University of North Carolina at Charlotte. He has translated Emmanuel Levinas's *Ethics and Infinity* (Duquesne University Press, 1985), *New Talmudic Readings* (Duquesne University Press, 1999), and *Time and the Other (and Additional Essays)* (Duquesne University Press, 1987). He is also the editor of *Face to Face with Lévinas* (SUNY Press, 1986) and the author of *Ethics, Exegesis, and Philosophy* (Cambridge University Press, 2001), among other books.

The University of Illinois Press
is a founding member of the
Association of American University Presses.

———————————————————————

Composed in 10.5/13 Adobe Minion
by Type One, LLC
for the University of Illinois Press
Manufactured by Thomson-Shore, Inc.

University of Illinois Press
1325 South Oak Street
Champaign, IL 61820-6903
www.press.uillinois.edu